D1757170

HAMMERSMITH AND FULHAM

3 8005 01506 552 2

Hedge
Britannia

Hedge Britannia

A Curious History
of a British Obsession

HUGH BARKER

BLOOMSBURY

LONDON · BERLIN · NEW YORK · SYDNEY

First published in Great Britain 2012

Copyright © 2012 by Hugh Barker

The moral right of the author has been asserted

Bloomsbury Publishing Plc, 50 Bedford Square, London WC1B 3DP
Bloomsbury Publishing, London, Berlin, New York and Sydney

A CIP catalogue record for this book is available from the British Library

ISBN 978 1 4088 0186 4

10 9 8 7 6 5 4 3 2 1

Designed and set by seagulls.net

Printed in Great Britain by Clays Ltd, St Ives Plc

www.bloomsbury.com/hughbarker

For Diane and Leah, with thanks for their patience on the many hedge-related trips, diversions and digressions.

Contents

Part Two: Growth and Conservation

Introduction
How I Learned to Stop Worrying and Love My Hedge

Sometime walking, not unseen,
By hedgerow elms, on hillocks green
L'ALLEGRO, *JOHN MILTON*

I grew up surrounded by hedges. I can still feel the scratches I received whilst rescuing errant tennis, cricket and bouncy balls from their twisted, thorny depths. I remember one long, hot summer that I spent constructing a den that extended through the trampled brambles into the lower branches of the hedge guarding the back garden. If I hadn't relied on cardboard boxes as my main building material, the complicated structure might even have survived the first rainfall of autumn.

Another childhood memory: a failed attempt to retrieve the school hamster, who escaped in the garden whilst billeted at our house over the Easter holidays and disappeared promptly into the nearest hedge, never to be seen again. We followed the noise of his rustling up and down the dense undergrowth for an hour or so, before losing the trail. I like to imagine he went on to find a happier life in the fields that lay beyond, although having grown up in captivity, he sadly may have lacked the know-how to escape the local cats and foxes.

I had a relatively sheltered childhood, but the lives of children everywhere revolve around the boundaries of their territory. It might be the railings of the local park, the hedges and stone walls of farmland, the local back alleys and concrete mazes of the inner city, the edge of the next field, or the humble garden hedge that defines the stage you live your life on. Boundaries, formal or informal, are among the first things we learn about our place in the world.

Children's books are often about magical transgressions of those boundaries. In the Narnia books, the Pevensey children escape from a house through a wardrobe, while in *Alice's Adventures in Wonderland,* Alice falls through 'a large rabbit-hole under the hedge'.* As children and adults, we want to feel safe and secure in our own space, but we also want to dream about fantastic adventures beyond.

Flying into the British Isles on an aeroplane today, there are two things you always notice. First there is the sheer depth of green in the land, a range of lush shades resulting from the fact that these are small, rain-buffeted islands off the western coast of Europe. It's a reminder that we should be eternally grateful for the Gulf Stream, which at least moderates the turbulent Atlantic weather patterns. Second, and more importantly, there is the traditional checkerboard pattern that is still so distinctive in the lowland countryside.

---

* 'It flashed across her mind that she had never before seen a rabbit with either a waistcoat-pocket, or a watch to take out of it, and burning with curiosity, she ran across the field after it, and fortunately was just in time to see it pop down a large rabbit-hole under the hedge.' The hedge is often incorrectly replaced by a tree in modern adaptations.

A patchwork of hedgerows.

It is a pattern of boundaries and barriers that breaks the land into individual parcels. Having grown up in Britain, that irregular geometric pattern always signifies 'home' to me, for better or worse. It also reveals a landscape that has been sub-divided by a million hedges over the course of history.

That pattern of enclosed patches of green isn't restricted to the countryside. I grew up in Burgess Hill, a town in the commuter belt, an hour on the main line from London. The morning train I caught to secondary school was packed with business types on their way to work in the city. I even seem to remember the occasional bowler hat, although I may just be reconstructing a cliché of Englishness learned from films such as *Mary Poppins*.

It was a typical southern town in many ways. Beyond the town centre, concrete multi-storey car park and marketplace, the streets and housing estates encroached gradually into the surrounding countryside. In the distance, the chalky South Downs were faintly visible. The majority of homes in the town, whether large or small, were set in their own patch of land, hemmed in by hedges and fences that created some degree of privacy and discouraged any intrusion by outsiders. This way of life seemed normal to me in my childhood. But the landscape didn't always look this way, either in town or country.

* * *

Hedges roughly divide the last millennium of British history into two halves. A rural, feudal society was gradually transformed into the nation of modern agriculture and industry. Enclosures (the conversion of open common land into private enclosed farmland) were created from at least the thirteenth century onwards, and were the cause of controversies and riots in Elizabethan times. But it was the changes of the eighteenth and nineteenth centuries that truly created the jigsaw landscape we recognise today.

At the peak of the main enclosures period, between 1750 and 1850, open fields and common land were divided into smaller, privately owned plots of land. Fast-growing shrubs such as blackthorn and hawthorn were planted to mark out the new plots, and as they twisted their roots deep into the soil, the huge unfenced fields that had formed much of the typical countryside scene gradually disappeared. Over 2,000 miles of hedge were planted each year during this period. If they had been planted in a straight line, this would have created a hedge that stretched around the world eight times. Rearing upwards in a vertical line, the hedge would almost have reached the moon. Many of those original hedges are still standing, testament to one of the biggest land-grabs in history.

This was the period when the balance between common land and exclusively private property was permanently transformed, as wealthy landowners protected their newly private land behind these hedges. As a result, many rural labourers lost their livelihoods and were forced to move to the burgeoning new towns. There they would find factories and mills providing employment for those who could work, and (eventually) workhouses for those who couldn't or wouldn't. Instead of a country of peasants we steadily became a nation of town and city dwellers.

The urban middle classes gradually became choked by the factory smoke, and repelled by the stench and proximity of the 'lower classes'. So they moved away from crowded town and city centres to the newly built suburbs. There, they chose to surround their precious gardens with hedges.

An Englishman's home is his castle, but rather than a moat, he has a hedge to keep the world at bay. In earlier centuries country dwellers huddled together for safety, from enemy attack or wild animals, behind stockades, dense hedges and trenches, and they held most of the space within the safety zone in common. The fact that people could now grow a modest hedge and assume that this polite indication of a boundary would repel invasion demonstrates how much those primal fears had been conquered.

Gardens and parks now came to be seen as tiny pieces of countryside, recreated as havens within the town. From

A recent example of idiosyncratic topiary
at the Oasis Café on Lindisfarne.

the eighteenth century onwards people who knew nothing about the real countryside started to hark back to the fictional rural utopia of 'Merrie England', seeing the country as an idyllic escape.*

And hedges became fodder for suburban eccentricity. The peculiar, ancient art of topiary had been revived in the English country house in the Renaissance period, and from there it spread to the urban environment. Bizarre creatures, columns and spirals sprouted from innocent garden hedges in towns and villages everywhere. Miniature hedge mazes were planted in civic parks and pleasure gardens. In the nineteenth and twentieth centuries, amateur gardeners vied to see who could invent the most insane topiary scheme on the street.

---

* While, as the Kingsley Amis character Jim Dixon points out in *Lucky Jim*, 'The point about Merrie England is that it was about the most un-Merrie period in our history'.

By this stage, hedges had become so commonplace we had almost stopped noticing how strange these developments were. When they weren't fulfilling the role of eccentric decorations, they were just boundary markers, which deterred undesirables from inadvertently setting foot within our space, and screened gardens from being observed by *hoi polloi.*

When hedges were noticed it was often because of the disputes they caused between neighbours. The twentieth century popularisation of the fast-growing leylandii (Leyland Cypress) exacerbated the tendency for hedges to become a focus of such disagreement because it grows to extraordinary heights, blocks light from neighbouring gardens and draws water greedily from the soil, thus blighting plant growth in the surrounding area.

Several groups have devoted themselves to battling owners who allow leylandii to grow too high – the pressure group Hedgeline was instrumental in lobbying the government for legislation regarding the arbitration process for excessively high hedges. At time of writing, the Scottish equivalent, ScotHedge, is involved in a long battle to have similar legislation adopted in Scotland, and there is also a campaign under way in Northern Ireland.

Sadly, as we shall see later in the book, the emotion aroused by leylandii means that some disputes have ended in violence and even death. Such tragedies are a living reminder that hedges can still mean much more than mere lines on a map.

* * *

When I was twelve, in the late 1970s, the hedge at the front of our house became the subject of a milder form of controversy.

In a street of regimented fences and well-kept gardens, our front hedge was at one point sufficiently unkempt to provoke a complaint from the residents' association. My father was furious at their interference, but he was also determined not to give them any further excuse for complaint.

A rota was drawn up, and I had to take a turn every third Saturday trimming the hedge back to a perfect, unnatural rectangle. I was unknowingly re-enacting a bastardised version of the ancient ritual of hedge trimming, carried out with billhooks and axes as a regular farming chore in centuries past. My father would look with bloody-minded pride at the sculpted right angles of the corners, which displayed an ironic compliance with a code of behaviour that he found absurd.

I've had a strange relationship with hedges ever since. For a long time when I was younger I only saw them as symbols of the suburban existence that I wanted to escape by moving to London. Then I gradually began to view them as remnants of the past that deserved closer attention.

In gardens, parks and countryside they are often the most humble element, easy to overlook. However they can be objects of great fascination in their own right. The nineteenth-century nature writer Richard Jefferies wrote of his daily observations of the Wiltshire hedgerows in *Field and Hedgerow*, saying:

The light is never the same on a landscape many minutes together, as all know who have tried, ever so crudely, to fix the fleeting expression of the earth with pencil. It is ever changing, and in the same way as you walk by the hedges day by day there is always some fresh circumstance of nature, the interest of which in a measure blots out the past.

Hedges can reveal a great deal not only about the history of a place, but also about the psychology of its current occupants. Suburban hedges can be rigidly shaped to the point of neurosis, sprawling messes, eccentric monuments and so much more besides. While in the countryside, the state of the hedges often depends on individual landowners, their finances and attitudes towards preservation. The old saying goes, 'When you meet a stranger, look at his shoes.' If you're on their home patch, it's not a bad idea to take a look at their hedge while you're at it.

Over time I became increasingly intrigued by what hedges tell us about the world we live in. Eventually I became a parent myself, and ended up moving back to a more suburban area on the remote fringes of London. There I entertained myself by trying to grow a miniature hedge to guard our section of garden from the neighbours' miniature dogs.

The hedge plants, which I bought from the local garden centre, were advertised as 'fast-growing'. I wanted a cheap solution, so I bought a set of five that would fill the required space, and settled back to watch the hedge expand. I was optimistically expecting something resembling a more manageable version of Sleeping Beauty's impenetrable barrier of thorns.

However, after three years the bushes have grown precisely five inches and are still a feeble imitation of a real hedgerow. The miniature dogs skip between them with impunity, and now I've got used to them roaming across my lawn from time to time when the mood takes them. Luckily, they are petrified of my cats' claws, and only visit when the cats are safely asleep inside, so the balance of power seems fairly even.

It is a preposterous hedge, but a weirdly satisfying one, since I grew it myself. Looking at it one day recently with a deep sense of ironic satisfaction I realised that I was steadily becoming more like my father than I had ever dreamt I would. As I speak to (and scold) my daughter, I hear nagging echoes of the way he used to talk to me. And for both my father and me, hedges became a channel for the ongoing struggle between conformity and non conformity. National and class identities are never simple equations based on origins – instead, we tussle with and react against the clichés of our youth, only to reappraise them as we age. Sometimes that suburban existence I so wanted to escape now seems a comforting return to my roots, while in other respects I still chafe at the idea of growing up and 'settling down'.

* * *

A fascination with hedges seems less peculiar now that they are in decline. As well as being a distinguishing feature of the landscape in town and country, hedges are a significant part of our ecological heritage. They have been described as 'linear woodland', because the very earliest hedges were created by simply leaving a border of trees and shrubs when a wooded area was cleared. Such assart hedges can still be observed in our countryside today.

In this way a remnant of the original forest* that covered the island was kept, and the indigenous bats, birds and insects

---

* The word 'forest' is a problematic one – as Oliver Rackham has sternly pointed out, historically it didn't mean woodland, but was the term used for enclosed hunting areas in the Norman period – a 'place of deer' rather than 'a place of trees'. However, it is in general use as a term for woodland, so I will risk using it that way.

were able to adapt their lifestyles to live in hedgerows rather than in woodland. Many species would have died out if the woodland destruction had not been partially balanced by hedgerow creation. Small mammals could take shelter or build homes in hedges, as well as using them as thoroughfares from one patch of woodland to another.

I live near to the North Circular Road, within a few miles of central London, but even here we regularly see a range of urban wildlife, including field mice, bats and foxes. London is a sprawling city but a remarkably green one, and occasional rural throwbacks flourish. Meanwhile, on the edges of most towns you find hedgehogs, foxes and even badgers scurrying through the garden hedges, the last urban survivors of the countryside menagerie. And throughout the countryside, hedgerows are a sanctuary or pathway for every kind of animal, from caterpillars and butterflies, pheasants and larks, weasels, stoats and voles to that violent little interloper, the mink that escapes from rural fur farms.

Since the 1950s there has been a steady destruction of hedgerows on farmland because of modern industrialised farming practices, with inevitable damage to the diverse range of wildlife and plant species that commonly resided there, to the point that parliament has had to pass legislation to protect them.

Even the dreaded leylandii are in decline. Pressure from Hedgeline and others led to the 2003 Anti-Social Behaviour Act including a special provision for dealing more stringently with high hedges. Hemmed in by the law on one flank, they are now being attacked on the other by disease. Cypress aphids have been breeding in increasing numbers and while no one knows the exact mechanism, leylandii that are attacked by the aphid wilt and turn an ugly shade of brown. Few would mourn them if they were to wilt into nothingness, but perhaps their plight is symbolic of a more widespread problem.

We are increasingly conscious of the importance of the hedgerow, and there are now organisations dedicated to protecting and replanting them. Scientists have devised a baffling variety of ways to study the ecological effects of a hedgerow. It is no longer legal to destroy them without permission, although the regulations governing planning are complex and confusing. It is not certain that the future of our hedgerows is safe, but at least there is a consciousness of their importance, and some political will at a national and local level to protect them.

In this book I will explore the state of the hedge today, and I'll relate this to the role of hedgerows in British history. I've been up and down the country, examining some fascinating hedges, lost villages and landscapes, and I've shared my obsessions with some of the people who, in one way or another, care for, nurture or write about hedges and hedgerows.

I've crawled into country hedgerows, stuck my head into neighbours' hedges, and wandered in country house mazes. I've talked to people with their own particular hedge passions, from horticultural experts to those who have become embroiled in hedge disputes, and from hedge-laying gurus to the Brixton man whose whale-shaped hedge was deemed unacceptable by the local council.

I want this book to be a series of rambles through geography and history, a light-hearted debate with the past about how it shaped the present. I want to consider the ways in which the hedge developed as a symbol of territory, boundary, property and decoration. Hopefully the resulting idiosyncratic guide to hedges will provide a glimpse into the mundane, eccentric and mixed-up place that is Britain today, and cast some light on how the hedge relates to the deep, tangled maze of our history.

Part One
ROOTS

Concerning the origins
of hedgelaying, formal
gardening and topiary

Preamble
Where is Britannia?

It is impossible for an Englishman to open his mouth,
without making some other Englishman despise him
PYGMALION, GEORGE BERNARD SHAW

Britain and 'Britishness' are perilous concepts, riddled with potential confusion and controversy. Before we start, I should apologise in advance for any irritation that may be caused if I sometimes seem to conflate 'English' with 'British' or 'Britain' with 'the British Isles'.

My own background means I know the most about the south-east and the north-west of England. I'm not certain whether I would describe myself as British, English or a Londoner (or even 'European'). It might depend on who I was talking to and whether I wanted to annoy them or not. For the most part, I have lived in suburbs and cities rather than the countryside, which colours my particular viewpoint.

Every part of the British Isles has its own history of gardens, landscape and urban growth. Offa's Dyke and Hadrian's Wall (and for a Cornish patriot, the River Tamar) are markers of national division, giant barriers dividing the land mass into separate countries, and other regions and counties have their own dividing lines. Ireland, or Eire, was relatively civilised during medieval England's dark ages, fell under the dominion of the British crown for centuries, and now has its independence. But while the Irish Sea divides Ireland from the rest of the British Isles, Northern Ireland remains part of the United Kingdom, albeit with greater self-determination than in the past. As a result, details of Irish history form part of the British story, although one could write an entirely different book about Irish hedges and land ownership (one in which the English would often deservedly be cast as villains).

In any case, the whole idea of a 'nation' is a fairly recent one. For a long time there was simply a network of local tribes, chieftains and warlords, sometimes at peace, sometimes at war. The monarchy was one centralised hierarchy (including individuals from other places such as the areas currently known as France, Germany and Holland) that managed to gain influence over these islands, and also land far beyond, at various times claiming tax and authority in France, in America, in India and beyond.

It has been a muddled state of affairs.

The name of 'The United Kingdom of Great Britain and Northern Ireland' suggests that Britain is the name for the island on which England, Scotland and Wales are situated. But historically there was no settled name for this island. Some ancient writers called it 'Britannia', while Pliny the Elder and others (including William Blake) have referred to the island as 'Albion', and to the surrounding islands as the 'Britanniae'. (Ireland's historic names included 'Ierne' (or 'Erin'), 'Scotia' and 'Hibernia'.)

It was James VI of Scotland, later James I of England, Wales and Ireland who revived the then archaic name of Britannia, declaring himself King of Great Britain in 1604 in an attempt to cement the Union of the Crowns. To the English parliament, he suggested the Union was the will of God: 'Hath He not made us all in one island, compassed with one sea and of itself by nature indivisible?'

You don't need to agree to recognise that there are many details regarding land ownership, agriculture and gardening that are common throughout Britain and the British Isles. For all their local variations and disputes, the old kingdoms and modern nations have a great deal of agricultural and horticultural history in common. For a start, it was often the same aristocracy that controlled land use and had the largest and most influential gardens and estates.

From William the Conqueror's gift of lands to his henchmen until the modern day you can trace unbroken lines of land ownership. When it comes to relations between the ruling class and the common people, you can see parallels between the Rebecca Riots and the Poll Tax uprisings, the Highland Clearances and the Potato Famine, the absentee landlords of Ireland and the landowners who enclosed land across other swathes of England, Scotland and Wales. So while we have to bear in mind the many local and national variations, large parts of hedge history are relevant to the British Isles as a whole.

I should also acknowledge that, while hedges are a very typical feature of British landscapes, they are found all over the world. And landscape and garden historians can point to other similarities across different cultures, for instance between British traditions of common land and the Japanese tradition of 'Satoyama' (a communal system that applied to the border land between the mountains and arable lowlands).

However, the story of hedges in other countries would tell us about different national stories, while only British hedges can tell us about the story of Britain.

1. Why, What and Wherefore
The Meaning of 'Hedge'

*From their high seat they could see over hedges into
buttercup meadows where cows lay munching the
wet grass and big cropping carthorses loomed out of
the morning mist. In one place the first wild roses were
out in the hedge and their father lassoed a spray
with his whip and passed it over his shoulder to Laura.*
LARK RISE TO CANDLEFORD, FLORA THOMPSON

First things first though: what exactly is a hedge? It may
seem a stupid question, but it is an unexpectedly hard
one to answer precisely. In the classic New Naturalist title
Hedges, the authors Hooper, Pollard and Moore wryly
acknowledge that they have actually spent most of the
chapter entitled 'What is a Hedge?' evading giving an answer
to the question.

The roots of the word 'hedge' are truly ancient. *Haga* (or
gehaeg or *hegge*) in Old English, *Hecke* in German and *haag*
in Dutch are etymologically connected words that originally
meant 'enclosure'. (Haga is also the old name for hawthorn,
whose name simply means 'hedge-thorn'.) Many British
place names incorporate Hay, Hays, Hayes, Hey, Haw, Haig,

'Hedge or Not?'

Undeniably a hedge.

An agricultural hedgerow.

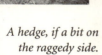

*A hedge, if a bit on
the raggedy side.*

*An ornamental row of trees.
Not a hedge.*

*A row of trees,
solid enough to
be called a hedge.*

*Might have to
phone a friend
about this one.*

*'When I grow up
I want to be a hedge'.*

*Hedge from
the waist up,
trees from the
waist down.*

23

Hague or Hough, which are variations of the same word, meaning either the hedge or the land enclosed by the hedge; for instance the name Hayward originates from the Norman name for the person who was tasked with looking after the hedges. In Welsh, Cae is similarly used for both the hedge and the field within.

If you ask people today what a hedge is you will get a bewildering variety of answers. Their image of a hedge will vary from the rural hedgerow through the ornamental hedge to the barriers of suburbia, and from the giant leylandii to the tiniest box edging. Some may not even realise that the basic species that make up hedgerows are trees rather than special 'hedge plants' or bushes, so it is worth mentioning that hedges are generally made up of trees or woody shrubs.

One simple dictionary definition is 'a line of closely planted shrubs or trees forming a barrier or boundary'. In English and Welsh case law, there is a more specific definition: 'a number of woody plants, whether capable of growing into trees or not, which are so planted as to be in line and which, when mature, to be so integrated together as to form both a screen and a barrier'. (This formed part of the judge's verdict in Stanton vs Jones, a landmark legal dispute between neighbours over the right to trim a high hedge – he also went on to note that a hedge needn't mark an exact boundary. See pages 191–2 for more detail.)

But even this degree of legal precision leaves ambiguities. When exactly does a line of trees become a hedge? How big can the gaps be before you stop calling it a hedge? If a hedgerow is neglected to the point that it is no longer recognisable as a hedge nor functioning as a barrier or screen, is it still at some metaphysical level a hedge?*

These questions matter when we come to look at the distinctions between farm hedges, garden hedges, ornamental hedges and other hedgelike objects. However, at this point I just want to focus on the idea that a hedge is almost always the result of human activity.

A random line of trees can't really be called a hedge. But what about a line of trees that have been intertwined by human hand to form a boundary, a row of shrubs that has been clipped into a regular shape, or spaced hawthorns that have been grown with the express intention of being laid as a hedge? Or an old hedge that has grown out and turned into a line of trees, which can still be perceived to be a hedge even if it has not functioned as one for years?

Any of these differing examples might reasonably be called a hedge. So for a clearer understanding of what hedges are, we need to consider both how and why they are created.

---

* Just to complicate matters, a recent DEFRA Hedgerow Survey Handbook gives an even more pedantic definition: 'A hedgerow is defined as any boundary line of trees or shrubs over 20m long and less than 5m wide at the base, provided that at one time the trees or shrubs were more or less continuous. It includes an earth bank or wall only where such a feature occurs in association with a line of trees or shrubs. This includes "classic" shrubby hedgerows, lines of trees, shrubby hedgerows with trees and very gappy hedgerows (where each shrubby section may be less than 20m long, but the gaps are less than 20m).' Perhaps we should just agree that there is no perfect definition …

The Creation of Hedges

Hedges come into existence in three main ways. They can be created as assart hedges, they can be planted hedges, or they can grow as fencerows.

Assart hedges

When an area of woodland is cleared of trees and turned into a field for cultivation, the resulting open area is an assart, or clearing. The trees that remained on the boundary of historic assarts were often turned into a hedge, which can be referred to rather beautifully as a 'woodland ghost' or more prosaically as a 'woodland relic' or 'assart hedge'. Such hedges preserve a tiny remnant of the dense woods that once covered the land, so they are our most ancient hedges, although the actual plants in the hedge may be distant descendants of the original plants.

These hedges are rather different from the planted hedges of later centuries, as they are significantly more likely to contain woodland tree species such as pry (small-leaved lime) or wild service, and to contain trees that rarely colonise planted hedges, such as hazel. They may also contain woodland plants such as bluebells, wood anemones or primroses* that have continued to reproduce within the hedge.

One example of this is in Dorset, where there is a markedly different pattern of primrose growth in the west and east of the county – in the west primroses are common in woods and

---

* 'Woodland ghost' can be used as a name for assart hedges, but it can also refer to these woodland plant species that survive in assart hedges.

hedges while in much of the east they are only found in woods. This probably reflects the distinction between the western area where many of the fields originated as assarts cleared from the forest, and the east where there was considerably more enclosure of open fields and commons in later centuries. The hedges of the west are thus far more likely to be relics of ancient woodland in which woodland plants have survived.

Thousands of assart hedges have been identified around the country. For example, in Hatfield Broadoak in Essex the modern hedges still follow the boundaries of an ancient forest of that name, which run along the parish boundaries. And at Shelley in Suffolk there is an unusual long hedge mostly made up of coppiced lime trees which is a remnant of nineteenth-century woodland clearance – the hedge runs exactly along the boundary of the lost Withers Wood.

Planted hedges

Trees and shrubs can be deliberately planted and cultivated as hedges, as we see on the boundaries of gardens, in features such as box edging and parterres or along the periphery of many agricultural fields.

The individual trees in a planted hedge can either be planted as saplings or grown from seed. In the fourth century BC, in his book on husbandry, Democritus recommended growing a hedge of brambles and whitethorn (hawthorn) by gathering the seeds of their fruit (as well as those of briars, gooseberries, barberries and others), preserving them in honey, then dipping a rope in the honey and burying it in a trench.

In Britain, it isn't always possible to reliably distinguish assart and planted hedges – in some cases suitable saplings

Saplings planted on a Hertfordshire
field boundary ready for future hedgelaying.

would have been dug up in local woodland and moved to
nearby fields to create a planted hedge, while assart hedges
can also contained planted specimens, since farmers would
transplant appropriate trees from elsewhere to bolster them.

The enclosures of the thirteenth to the nineteenth centuries
relied on cultivated hedges, often blackthorn and hawthorn
saplings, which were planted for their speed of growth, and
many of our surviving hedgerows were created in this period.

If an existing hedge is left untended, the growth at ground
level becomes sparse and a 'lollypopping' effect takes over: the
hedge plants become more tree-like, and the hedge becomes
ineffectual as a barrier. For this reason, hedges need regular
maintenance, however they were created.

The traditional techniques by which a row of trees can be
maintained as a compact barrier and kept to a manageable

height are 'pollarding', 'coppicing' and 'hedgelaying'. Pollarding is cutting trees back to the desired height to encourage horizontal growth. Coppicing is cutting trees right down to a stump, from which new growth is expected. And hedgelaying is a more complex method, whereby trees are cut and laid diagonally before being woven into a barrier (see chapter 3 for more detail).

Fencerows

Hedges can grow without being deliberately cultivated where there is protection from a fence, ditch or bank. In this case the young plants survive in the shelter, protected from the elements and the animals, and a hedgerow will result. For instance, on Dartmoor gorse hedges have grown along the lines of ancient, dilapidated stone walls. There are also miles of such hedgerows in areas of America such as Texas where

A lollypopped hedge, and some sheep.

farms have been abandoned and the fencing left behind – these can simply be called 'hedgerows' but I prefer to use the common American name for such a hedge, which is 'fence-row', to distinguish them more clearly from planted hedges.*

Another type of fencerow arises when a climbing plant such as ivy takes over an old fence or wall. In *Flora Britannica* Richard Mabey reports a case where ivy that was originally planted to cover a fence has, in the long run, taken over and is now holding the fence up, creating a kind of ivy hedge.

A fencerow grows without direct human intention – but it is none the less usually dependent on the creation of some kind of barrier that allows the hedgerow to flourish, and thus is still an indirect result of human shaping of the landscape.

So when we talk about a hedge we are almost always talking about a product of human activity, rather than a naturally occurring phenomenon. In ancient history, it was only once mankind started to shape and clear the landscape that hedges could come into being.

This implies that for any given hedge, there is a reason or reasons why that hedge exists. It doesn't make much sense to ask *why* a forest tree or a wild flower has grown. But cultivated nature, hedges included, can be viewed as the outcome of human intention – meaning we can try to understand the underlying reasons and purposes.

In other words, we can look at a hedge and ask *why?*

---

* Thoreau speaks of fencerows in his journal: 'It is only necessary that man should start a fence that Nature should carry it on and complete it. The farmer cannot plow quite up to the rails or wall which he himself has placed, and hence it often becomes a hedgerow and sometimes a coppice.'

The Uses of Hedges

This leads on to the next basic question – what are hedges for?
The short answer is that there are three main practical uses of
hedges – as barriers, boundaries and screens – and they can
also be grown for purely ornamental reasons.

Hedges as barriers

The earliest historical use of hedging was almost certainly as a
barrier, to keep animals in or intruders out, or for protection
from the elements. The first agricultural enclosures would
have been protected by fences, palisades or hedges. Whole
settlements would also have been enclosed for protection in
some areas of the world. The African 'zareba' – a thorn hedge
that surrounds a camp or enclosure – is one example of the
use of hedging for this purpose.

In Britain, hedges have been cultivated as barriers between
fields and gardens from time immemorial. They were used to
corral livestock and for protection from wild animals. Human
predators can be kept out by them too, as William Cobbett
pointed out in *The English Gardener*: 'four feet of good thorn-
hedge will keep the boldest boy from trees loaded with fine
ripe peaches; ... and if it will do *that*, nothing further need be
said in its praise.'*

Thorny or prickly plants, such as the vicious brambles
that colonise rural hedgerows, have often been used to reinforce barrier hedges. In Greek legend, Ardiaeus the tyrant

---

* My wife tells me that when she was young, a nearby house achieved the same
effect with more humour – the owner kept the children out very effectively with
a BEWARE OF THE SNAKES sign.

of Pamphylia was sentenced to be punished by being dragged backward and forward through a hedge of thorns. Today in Mexico tightly planted rows of cactuses are used to create a similarly terrifying obstacle.

Where hedges were created to contain animals, they often also incorporated an earth bank, and ditches on one or both sides, as these increased their effectiveness as a barrier. (The bank itself is referred to as a 'hedge' in some areas, even if it doesn't have plants on the top.)

Julius Caesar gives us the first recorded use of hedges as a military barrier, describing the tactics used by the Belgic tribes in using their prickly agricultural hedges as obstacles, from behind which they attempted to resist the cavalry attacks of his army in Gaul, en route to Britain. (Caesar describes the hedges as military barriers, but it seems more likely that they were agricultural hedges that the tribes used as improvised defences when they came under attack.)

The hedgerows of the same region became significant barriers to advancing Allied troops in the summer of 1944 following the D-Day landings. In the Cotentin area, they faced intense German resistance amidst difficult terrain composed of small fields and orchards. The conflict became known as the 'hedgerows war' or the 'battle of the *bocage*' (the French name for hedgerow).

The ancient hedgerows of the Cotentin were up to five metres high, having been neglected during the years of occupation. Dense barriers of hawthorn, blackthorn, hazel and brambles were interspersed with apple and pear trees, grown for calvados, pommeau and local ciders. They created perfect defensive fortifications. Ground troops could not see if a tank or self-propelled gun was waiting for them through the *bocage*, and the Germans could cut small holes in order to see attackers coming and set up ambushes.*

Tanks were unable to penetrate the dense hedgerows – driving into one was reportedly like driving a car into a brick wall. American troops experimented with flamethrowers and commandos with explosive devices, both with limited success. Eventually they improvised cutting attachments by fixing blades to their tank wheels in order to slash their way through.

Domestic hedges can also come under attack. There was a more comical case of hedgebreaking in the seventeenth century when Peter the Great stayed in the diarist John Evelyn's house in Deptford. He was there to study shipbuilding on the adjacent Thames dockyards, but was prone to throwing parties back at the house. Evelyn, a devoted gardener, was especially proud of his holly hedges and was appalled to discover that the Tsar had been playing drunken games in which a servant pushed him in a wheelbarrow through not only the flowerbeds, but also the hedges.

Happily the hedges recovered from any damage inflicted – soon afterwards Evelyn wrote:

Is there under heaven a more glorious and refreshing object of the kind, than an impregnable Hedge a hundred and sixty feet in length, and seven feet high, and five in diameter, which I can shew in my poor Gardens at any time of the year, glittering with its armed and vernish'd leaves?

---

* Hedges were used in the same way by musketeers in the English Civil War.

The taller Standards at orderly distances blushing with their natural Corall. It mocks at the rudest assaults of the Weather, Beasts, and Hedgebreakers.

In some parts of Britain today, hedge diving (throwing yourself into a hedge) and hedge hopping (jumping a series of back garden hedges as though you are in a steeplechase) are popular sports with a certain kind of drunken teenager. I couldn't possibly condone such vandalistic behaviour, or dignify it by suggesting that a brief internet search might bring up some amusing videos of these activities.

Hedges as boundaries

Hedges have been used throughout British history to mark out the ownership and division of land. Many of today's parish boundaries have been in place for over a thousand years. The Anglo-Saxon charters, which delineated the ownership of ancient estates, often referred to hedges, ditches and earth banks, and in some cases these would have been features of the landscape that were established in the Roman period or even earlier. To this day you can walk the boundaries of some of these estates by following the directions, observing the banks, riverbeds and natural phenomena that were used to define the territory of the landowner.*

A later example comes from a seventeenth-century account of the parish bounds of Breocke in Cornwall:

---

* In his classic *The Making of the English Landscape*, W. G. Hoskins writes: 'I believe in general that *boundaries* are one of the most ancient features in the English landscape – parish, county, hundred, estate'.

> Hedges are sufficient bounds between the lands of our parish and certane lands belonging to St Issey from a place called Pynxkin lyeng upon the shoare of the great River of Allen to No mans land and from thence to a yet [gate] called Floud yet.

Near Flittermere Pond in Cambridgeshire, a hedge marks the location of an ancient controversy. 'Flittermere' is derived from the Anglo-Saxon words *flitter* (dispute) and *gemere* (boundary) – the pond would once have been held in common between several parishes but at some point it was taken into the Great Gidding parish and a hedge marked the boundary. Whether this hedge was the cause of the boundary dispute, or the means by which it was settled, is lost to history.

In Ireland, hedges were planted to enclose 'town lands' from the medieval period onwards. Known as townland boundaries, these are some of the most ancient Irish hedges. They also tend to be the most species-rich hedges, so their conservation is a matter of importance. A recent survey of hedgerows in County Monaghan, an inland county in the province of Ulster, found that 12 per cent of them formed part of a townland boundary. More importantly it showed that where townland boundary hedges linked into native woodland they were significantly more likely to have a rich variety of species, including plant species less common in other hedges such as wood sorrel, ground ivy and hedge woundwort.

Hedges as screens
The first specific literary reference to a hedge is probably in Homer's *Odyssey*, when he describes the garden of Alcinous, the Phaiakian king:

Close to the gates a spacious garden lies,
  From storms defended, and inclement skies;
  Four acres was the allotted space of ground,
  Fenced with a green enclosure all around.

The island concerned was perhaps Corfu, although there
are the inevitable academic niggles about the exact location.
Homer gives a detailed description of the fruits and vegetables that were cultivated within this enclosed garden, and
seems greatly impressed by the wealth and horticultural skill
that these demonstrate.*

Hedges can be used as screens in various ways. They can
function as windbreaks, as in the traditional daffodil fields of
the Isles of Scilly, where the flowers were protected from fierce
Atlantic winds in tiny fields surrounded by dense, tall hedges.
Shade-loving plant species may also flourish next to a stra-
tegically positioned hedge. And in a garden or rural setting,
hedges can be used to create privacy or to split an open space
into separate divisions.

The seclusion afforded by hedges has encouraged the use
of gardens as places of love and flirtation. In the fifteenth-
century work *Hypnerotomachia Poliphili*, Francesco Colonna
describes a garden within which nymphs pay tribute to Cupid.
It is guarded by a dense bushy hedge of myrrh, so thick it can't
be seen through.

---

* Horace Walpole points out this was not a grand garden by modern standards:
'As late as Homer's age an enclosure of four acres, comprehending orchard,
vineyard and kitchen-garden, was a stretch of luxury the world at that time had
never beheld'. (*On Modern Gardening: Ancient Gardens*)

The ladies of early wealthy Egyptian households were secluded from worldly temptation in shaded courtyards, fringed with sycamores, fig trees, date palms and pomegranate trees, and later harems and pleasure grounds in the East often lay within hedged or walled enclosures.* In the medieval period, European gardens often included 'pleasaunces', private screened areas which were designed for entertainments, and to please the senses rather than for growing useful plants. Henry II reportedly took the pleasure garden a stage further when he built a hedge maze at Woodstock, with a hedged arbour at the centre, designed for trysts with his mistress Rosamund Clifford. (This might be apocryphal, but it was a well-known anecdote that helped to popularise hedge mazes in subsequent centuries.)

On a less romantic level, the modern suburban garden uses hedges of species such as privet, yew and box to create a sense of privacy even in densely populated areas. Roads and railways are also often screened by hedges, which absorb sound as well as blocking unwanted views.

Concealment can be used for more nefarious purposes. In Surrey recently, Robert Fidler used a dry hedge of hay bales to hide his illegally built mock Tudor castle-style house. Since no one objected to the building for four years after completion, the law would theoretically have allowed him to keep it. Rather unsportingly, the judge rejected this theory on the basis that the building hadn't technically been completed

---

* In *The One Thousand and One Nights*, Scheherazade's plight derives from Shahriyar's earlier discovery of his wife's tryst with a slave whilst bathing in the enclosed garden.

until the screen was removed, and ordered that the house should be demolished.

Ornamental hedges

Barriers, boundaries and screens represent the practical side of hedgemaking. But hedges have also been used throughout history as ornamental elements in gardens and parks. From knot gardens and parterres to hedge topiary and mazes, hedging has played an important role in modern garden design.

The development of ornamental gardens in a society is a sign that it has risen above the subsistence level of farming and acquired the capacity to undertake more frivolous forms of cultivation. So ornamental gardens have often been associated with wealth, luxury and privilege, although there are humbler examples of decorative hedges to be found in many ordinary gardens.

When considering the purpose of hedges it is important to look at both the practical and ornamental aspects. For an agricultural hedgerow, function tends to be more important than appearance; a garden hedge is often a marriage between the practical and decorative; while hedging or topiary in a formal garden can be purely ornamental.

The Language of Hedges

Most landscapes in the British Isles contain man-made elements, even in areas of apparent wilderness. Even on the remote slopes of Snowdonia where the rocky scenery is reminiscent of an untouched moonscape you can find stone walls, scars of old quarrying and roads through the passes. The same is true of the Highlands of Scotland, the peaks of the Pennines or the Mountains of Mourne, while on Dartmoor the industrial remains of the tin mining criss-cross the landscape.

Human activity was more intensive in the lowlands. Many fens and water meadows are the result of ancient drainage or irrigation projects, while the Norfolk Broads were formed by peat extraction in the Middle Ages, with the resulting holes having flooded in later centuries. From Neolithic times onwards the Peak District was deforested for agricultural purposes using techniques ranging from slash and burn to grubbing out, while the New Forest was cultivated as a hunting ground for William the Conqueror. Coppiced oaks in the Quantocks are an indication of early woodland industry, while ancient thoroughfares such as the Icknield Way and Watling Street can still be traced today.

From assart hedges to ancient boundaries, and from abandoned farmland to ornamental gardens, hedges played their role in the creation of this landscape. When we view them as meaningful historical artefacts that teach us about our past, we are not engaged in a mystical activity like trying to read tea leaves in a cup. It is more like studying the lines and marks on the face of an octogenarian, or the comments in the margin of a library book.

Every hedge tells a story, tragic or comic, ancient or modern. But in order to understand what hedges can tell us about our country, we need to learn the language of hedges. We need to work out the grammar and vocabulary of this language and use it to interpret what we see.

2. Monks Wood
The Great British Hedgerow Experiment

Present generations of farmers and tax payers have an
important holding operation to perform; we should hang on
to those features of the landscape whose value will increase
with the years and which will be increasingly appreciated.
This should include plenty of good British hedges.
HEDGES, E. POLLARD, M. D. HOOPER, N. W. MOORE

It's a chilly December day in Huntingdonshire. There is always something mournful about this part of the country in winter. The flat fields stretch off towards fenland in the north and east, while the A1 drones past in the distance carrying traffic from London up to Lincolnshire, Yorkshire and Scotland beyond. There is a low mist hanging over the lowland ponds and streams. A pheasant stares at me from the middle of a waterlogged field.

On the way here, I passed Grafham Water, a reservoir beneath which up to twenty miles of drowned hedges lie, lost with the fields when the gentle valley was flooded. The flat landscape of Huntingdonshire and neighbouring Cambridgeshire is relieved by occasional higher points, such as the Isle of Ely, but much of it is beneath sea level, protected by the surrounding land mass from permanent inundation.

The wind that blows in from the North Sea and the Baltic and Scandinavian nations beyond is bitter in the winter months. But in spite of the cold and the lack of hills it can be a beautiful place, with huge, dizzying skies emphasised by the wide vistas below.

My destination is Monks Wood, an ecological research station that was founded here by the government body Nature Conservancy in the early 1960s, on heavy clay fields adjoining an ancient piece of woodland. This redoubtable institution did a great deal for British ecology, and for rural hedges in particular.

At that time hedgerows were in serious decline. After the Second World War, the aim for agriculture was efficiency, as the government sought self-sufficiency in food. This was an understandable reaction to the shortages of the war and the years of rationing. However, the practical result was a kind of agricultural brutalism, a rural parallel to the ugly concrete blocks that were being erected in the cities. Thousands of miles of hedges were torn up each year, fallow moors and heaths were drained and ploughed to create massive fields, and the old ways of husbanding the land were forgotten as mechanical farming techniques were adopted.

Farmers had traditionally seen themselves as custodians of the countryside, but now they had to prioritise greater productivity. In addition they were subjected to bewildering regulations that gave them one grant to destroy a hedgerow and another to plant a new one.

However, a few voices started to be heard raising concerns about the ecological consequences of these changes. Dr N. W. Moore, the first director of Monks Wood, was an early advocate of the idea that hedgerows, and the countryside in general, were being damaged by post-war agriculture, both in the extensive use of pesticides and in new techniques such as machine-cutting of hedges using a flail. In order to take a closer scientific look at this question, he had a series of experimental hedgerows planted in the heavy clay of the Huntingdonshire fields. The strips were carefully measured in imperial units, each strip a set number of chains* in length, with the original shrubs planted in equidistant spacing.

He was joined at Monks Wood by Dr Max Hooper and Dr E. Pollard, who in 1974 would become his co-authors on *Hedges*, a book that has near-biblical status for hedgerow enthusiasts. Along with their fellow scientists they worked on a series of experiments and investigations into the management of the hedgerows, and the preservation and nurturing of the plants and animals that either lived in or visited the hedges.

They also took their work out into the field, measuring hedges around the land, traversing the countryside on branch railways to observe field patterns, and using sources such as the aerial photographs taken by the Luftwaffe in the war to support their findings. (Hitler's desire for a good record of the country he intended to invade meant that this was the most comprehensive aerial imaging available at the time.)

It was Max Hooper who gave his name to 'Hooper's Law', a method by which approximate dating of hedgerows can be attempted. At its simplest, the law is based on a count of

---

* A chain is twenty-two yards, the length of a cricket pitch. There are ten chains in a furlong (a 'furrow long', the standard old field length) and eight furlongs in a mile. Hedges were traditionally measured in chains.

the number of woody species (trees or shrubs) found in a 100-foot length of hedge. The number of species (averaged over three or more sample stretches) multiplied by 100 gives a rough estimate of the age of the hedge. So a hedge with an average of five woody species might be tentatively dated to the sixteenth century. (Hooper's Law is a rule of thumb rather than a precise tool and should only be used alongside other dating techniques such as local history, old maps, study of the field patterns, other flora in the hedge and so on.)

This focused attention on the fact that hedgerows can be ancient monuments, redolent with local history, and that some are remnants of the original wildwood, having been left in place when the trees were cleared to create fields. It had frequently been assumed that the hedgerows that were being destroyed in this period were of little historic interest, being a century or two old at most. Hooper's Law helped remind people that many hedges were far more ancient parts of the local environment, dating back to the Middle Ages, the Romans, or even to the Bronze Age. (Of course, the fact that a hedge is a thousand years old or more doesn't mean that the individual plants within it are of the same age, only that there has been continuous growth and regrowth on that site.)

One good example ran along the border of Monks Wood itself – the long, undulating hedgerow known as Judith's Hedge, which Hooper demonstrated had been continuously present since the Norman period (Judith was a niece of William the Conqueror).

The academic work on hedges at Monks Wood became a catalyst in the gradual revision of post-war attitudes towards hedges. Hedgerow maintenance had been an ancient craft, with plants traditionally cut by hand in annual cycles. The increased mechanisation of agriculture in the post-war period meant that centuries of accumulated hedge lore was becoming either lost or irrelevant.

Many hedges that were machine-cut with flails started to show signs of decline. Previously, hedges had been kept healthy by the farmworkers, who allowed them to grow incrementally larger over the years and judged the trimming carefully. By cutting throughout the hedge they encouraged new growth at ground level and kept the hedge in good condition. However, if hawthorn hedges are machine cut at the same height each year, the plants become stressed as the new growth is repeatedly cut. Stems become twisted and gnarled and the hedge becomes unhealthy and gappy as a result. To address these problems, government policy on agricultural grants and recommendations needed to be changed.

Damage caused by flail-cutting a blackthorn hedge.

Monks Wood was only one part of the movement to preserve hedgerows. There was widespread concern amongst farmers, rural campaigners and others that the country was being modernised out of recognition. But the hard, patient work of the Monks Wood scientists helped to make an impact on the distant mandarins of Whitehall, changing official policy, and thus slowing down the rate of destruction of the hedgerows.

When I first explored the idea of visiting Monks Wood to see the experimental hedges, now nearly fifty years old, I was sorry to discover that the research station had closed down in January 2009. The Byzantine politics of the competition for research funds between various universities and institutes, together with internal expenditure cuts, had led to its closure. More in hope than expectation, I contacted former staff members in the hope of finding out more. And serendipitously, it turned out that I hadn't missed my chance after all.

Tim Sparks, who looked after the hedgerow experiments for the best part of a decade before the centre closed, is still returning to the site. A phenologist* who is now working as a visiting professor to Poznan University of Life Sciences in Poland, he has been measuring and photographing the trees and hedges on the same day every year over an extended period and the closure of the station hasn't prevented him from continuing with these experiments for as long as he can.

He has offered to give me a guided tour.

---

* Phenology is the natural study of the times of recurring natural phenomena, such as when birds migrate, leaves fall, and so on, especially in relation to climate. (I know because I had to look it up before I met Tim.)

The Experimental Hedges

The early brightness has faded into a cloudier day when Tim greets me at the deserted site. He is dryly amused by my townie shoes, which will clearly be inadequate to the task of keeping feet dry and warm in muddy fields which have been generously manured by the cows and horses who wander them. In return I am rather envious of his woollen socks and Wellingtons.

We start at Saul's Drive, an old green lane leading into the wood. The fact that it has a name which refers to a former denizen of the woods is a sign of its antiquity. The green lane is fringed by two mature hedgerows, with slight ditches to the sides.

Tim describes such green lanes as a 'linear hotspot for biodiversity'. This is because the hedgerows on either side often date to the creation of the lane from woodland and thus contain an abundance of species, including plants and trees normally only found in woodland. As a result, they provide food and shelter to a wide variety of animal species.

From Saul's Drive we walk along a muddy path and through the gate with a 'Beware of the Bull' warning (Tim assures me the bull is a friendly one). Beyond the gate we reach the fields containing the experimental hedgerows.

The first field contains the original nine hedges, stretching magnificently across the field in parallel lines. They have the look of the countryside hedgerows we know so well, except for their symmetry and the fact that they do not reach the ends of the field, leaving a space for us to walk around the ends of each row.

Saul's Drive.

These hedges are made up of hawthorn, easily the most common agricultural hedgerow species in Britain. There are actually two wild varieties (along with occasional hybrids between the two): common hawthorn, *Crataegus monogyna*, and Midland hawthorn, *Crataegus laevigata*. *Monogyna* is the species commonly cultivated and planted in hedges, while *laevigata* is found mainly in woods.

Hawthorn hedgerow in the winter, Monks Wood.

Tim explains that the current experiments on these hawthorn hedges are measuring the yield of leaves and berries under various management regimes. Some sections have simply been cut back, while others have been subjected to hedgelaying. The maintenance is variously carried out in one-, two- or three-year cycles.

I love the dark red hawthorn berries that bring clouds of colour to country lanes at this barren time of the year. But, more importantly, for many birds they are an essential, if unexciting part of the winter diet (Tim describes their nutritional content as being the bird's equivalent of a bowl of dry Weetabix). Annual cutting severely restricts growth of these berries as they will only grow on two-year-old wood, which is why cutting in a two- or three-year cycle has become a standard recommendation. The Monks Wood research has also recently shown that cutting in winter allows a much higher yield of berries than cutting in the autumn.

On the hedges, you can clearly see the separate sections that have been cut in different ways. Some are thick with berries, while others show a more paltry crop. One hedgerow is almost bare wood until the bit of tape marking a new section, at which point it bursts out into a much bushier, leafier form. (A wood pigeon has chosen to build its nest in the most exposed section, providing evidence for Tim's suggestion that they aren't the brightest of birds.)

Further along we reach a field where the scientists went on to plant a series of hedges of different species for further experiments. There has been less experimental work done on them recently so they are not as well maintained as the hawthorn hedges.

The original plan was to have a row for each of the British hedgerow species most commonly found on farms. The species the scientists chose were: hazel, elm, field maple, hornbeam, beech, blackthorn, buckthorn and holly (although the latter two didn't survive here). In addition they planted two mixed hedges – one of beech and hawthorn, and one that was a mix of many species.

A few of these hedgerows were unfortunately dug up later to create an area for the study of rabbits, which is an odd story in its own right. A watchtower was built from which scientists and students took turns observing the behaviour of the rabbits. As we walk through the mud, Tim tells me the story of the enclosure, which the scientists nicknamed Stalag Bun. The rabbits spent their lives in carefully segregated runs, with wire fencing dug into the ground, and metal plates to deter predators such as stoats and weasels.

After the end of these experiments, the runs were breached, and the rabbits escaped from their prison and colonised the local area – I twist my foot in at least one warren entrance as we are exploring. Stalag Bun itself has been reinvaded by elms and blackthorns, both of which are capable of suckering, reproducing from the remains of roots. And along the wire fencing, new hedges have grown up, fencerows arising naturally where the young woody plants are protected from animals and the elements. So, having lost the first battle, the hedges won out over the rabbits in the long run.

The Spread of Woodland Species

The way trees multiply was also studied at Monks Wood. There are two wilderness areas that at first sight appear to be mere scrubland. But in fact they are carefully measured out, in order to assess the speed at which tree species spread from the woodland of Monks Wood.

When Hooper's Law gives us a useful estimate of the age of a hedge, it is because of the specific ways that tree species reproduce. In general, trees spread at a fairly slow rate so hedges are only gradually colonised by them.

Tree species have different ways of reproducing, and the method of reproduction defines the speed at which they can spread. Some, such as the wild service tree, rarely reproduce from seed in the British climate, and thus only reproduce by suckering. This makes them rare outside of ancient woodland. Others, such as hawthorn, spread when birds eat berries and excrete the seeds. These species can easily jump as far as a bird's territorial flights will carry them. Oaks are also spread by birds, although in their case it is usually because jays like to stash acorns away for later and, in the manner of a squirrel forgetting where it has buried its nuts, sometimes fail to return to collect their meal. Another group, including ash and willow, spread through wind dispersal of their seeds, meaning they can leapfrog across the countryside in uneven jumps.

Some species use more than one form of dispersal. Blackthorn, which has spread throughout the Monks Wood wilderness areas, reproduces by both suckering and seed dispersal by birds. It is a species with wicked thorns, capable of piercing a Wellington boot (and, when planted around enchanted castles, of deterring all but the most determined of princes). It's not surprising that farm animals choose to give it a wide berth, making it a rather effective stock-proof plant.

At the far end of the wilderness area we reach Judith's Hedge. One of the fascinating things about this hedge is that one section of it was straightened and replanted in the nineteenth century, while the two curving sections on either side of the Victorian section are of much older provenance, dating back to the Norman period. They seem to have been originally formed as woodland relics on the edges of an assart.

(As a rule of thumb, straight hedges tend to be more recent than curving ones. Hedges from the eighteenth century onwards, especially enclosure hedges, were often straight, while earlier fields were cleared and enclosed in a more piecemeal way and the boundary hedges would often jag to and fro to include large boulders or trees within the hedge, in order to make the clearance of the land easier.)

Tim points out several signs of antiquity in the older sections. At one point we encounter a wild service tree – it is too far from the woods to have spread here by suckering, so it is a clear sign that this is indeed a relic of ancient woodland. The berries of the wild service are called chequers – they are slightly shrivelled and unappetising in appearance, although they were apparently used to flavour beer (this being one suggested explanation of the common British pub name 'The Chequers').

On the ground inside the hedge there is a patch of dog's mercury, which spreads very slowly, and in this part of the country is only found in ancient woodland. The hedge also contains several beautiful sprays of spindle, a woodland margin plant that produces vivid pink berries at this time of year, as well as species such as dogwood and maple.

By comparison to the ancient section, the Victorian stretch of the hedge contains relatively few species. There are some colonisers – for instance we see a wild privet* tree in this section of the hedge. There are also examples of dog rose, ash and sycamore – but the make-up is clearly less diverse than the more ancient stretches.

However, one of the early experiments at Monks Wood observed a fascinating phenomenon. The woodland plant species were creeping ever so slowly from the ancient sections of the hedge into the Victorian section. Year by year, the dog's mercury, bluebells and wood anemones inched their way along the hedges, living proof of the theory that hedgerows are a form of 'linear woodland'.

* * *

---

* This is related to the shorter-leaved variety of privet which is so common in British garden hedges.

Many of the other patient, fascinating and occasionally bizarre experiments that were carried out here over the years are recorded in *Hedges*. It is a treasure trove of fascinating information on the flora and fauna that can be found in hedgerows at various times of the year; the way that hedge density affects wind speed and temperature in the lee of the wind; and the distance from a hedge at which birds tend to congregate, among other subjects.

Some of the detail is highly technical and of interest largely from an agricultural or scientific point of view. But throughout the experiments recorded here and elsewhere there is a common thread, which is the crucial role hedges play in sustaining the biodiversity of the environment. A wide variety of flora and fauna finds shelter and sustenance in hedgerows. Even the later hedgerows that contain fewer species are vibrant habitats and the countryside would be a far more barren place if the post-war removal of hedges had continued to accelerate.

For their preservation we have to thank a loose alliance of farmers, scientists, environmentalists and rural organisations. Monks Wood played its own significant part in that process. There are still threats to rural hedgerows today, but things could have been much worse if agricultural policy had remained unchanged.

The story of Monks Wood isn't quite over. The woodland will still be open to the public. Tim will be back on the same day next year photographing the same trees for his research. The fields containing the hedges will be owned by Natural England and the current experiments on the hawthorn hedges will continue at least for the two remaining years of their current cycle. But we have lost an important institution in the battle to save our future hedgerows.

As Tim and I reach the end of our tour, we take a moment to pay our respects. For a brief moment, standing by the silent, deserted buildings I can't help feeling like we are the last two people at a wake.

The very existence of these experimental hedges always suggested that, as a nation, we were conscious of the importance of hedges in our landscape and environment. If Monks Wood is no more, let's hope it doesn't mean we are losing that awareness, and that we will still cherish our hedges in the future as we have in the past.

The Elephant Hedge

Here tulips bloom as they are told;
Unkempt about those hedges blows
An English unofficial rose ...
'THE OLD VICARAGE, GRANTCHESTER', RUPERT BROOKE

One of the most spectacular and weird hedges I have ever had the pleasure of encountering is the Elephant Hedge at Rockingham Castle.

Perched on a natural escarpment above the Welland Valley, Rockingham was built on the instructions of William the Conqueror and has been owned and gradually rebuilt by one family (the Watsons) for the best part of five centuries, since the crown relinquished it in the sixteenth century. The castle is an accumulation of different periods of architecture, with a heavy dose of Tudor.

Stern battlements give way on one side to a beautiful terraced lawn with views across the Midland countryside below. From there you can observe the typical local patterns of enclosed pastures, with white sheep dotting the green grass and darker hedges marking the field boundaries. It is easy to imagine the lawn hosting croquet games, with cucumber sandwiches and tea served in china cups.

Dividing this lawn from a formal garden area is the massive Elephant Hedge. It is a strange structure made up of smoothly trimmed, undulating curves that could be taken to suggest

The Elephant Hedge.

the monumental curves of elephants' bodies. It is divided into two parallel sections, with a shaded walkway concealed in between, and an entrance halfway down the lawn side through which you can enter its depths.

On closer examination, I'm not sure that it bears any clear resemblance to elephants at all, apart from one small section at the end, which could be taken for a figurative depiction of a single animal if you squint at it. As a whole, the hedge looks more like a cloud formation, or possibly a growth of mushrooms in the damp wood of a fallen forest tree.

Perhaps because it doesn't have the formality of old-fashioned topiary, the Elephant Hedge strikes me as rather unnatural. Of course, that is a peculiar word to apply to something that is made of trees. But any wildness they once possessed has been tamed in the transformation into this strangely shaped phenomenon.

I am visiting the castle with my seven-year-old daughter. She literally falls down laughing on her back when she comes around the corner and first sees the hedge. There is indeed something very humorous about it. It looks a marvellous place for children to play, but otherwise it doesn't have any obvious use. It must be a purely ornamental feature, if a rather odd one.

Head gardener Richard Stribley is cutting the lawns around the battlemented hedge enclosure on the site of an older formal garden. He pauses long enough to tell me that the Elephant Hedge was created in the days of John Watson, 450 years ago. There was a minor craze for elephants at the time. The Roman army of Claudius brought a fighting specimen to terrify the locals, but after that there were no elephants in Britain until Louis IX of France gave one to Henry III of England in 1255. It lived on roast beef and red wine at the Tower of London, eventually dying as a result of this overindulgence. In the sixteenth and seventeenth century elephants were a rare sight in Britain – most people's knowledge of them came from anatomically inaccurate drawings and exotic exaggerations. The hedge may well have been designed by someone who had never seen an elephant in the flesh.

During the English Civil War, the castle was taken over by Cromwell's Roundheads and subsequently suffered a Royalist siege, but the hedge was spared. Ever since it has been tended by the gardeners of Rockingham, and this beautiful location has retained its idyllic air through all the wars and upheavals of the intervening years. I find that a rather soothing image, reminiscent of Rupert Brooke's wartime reveries of the broken clock at Grantchester.

Not all great homes were as lucky. Many of the great Victorian gardens fell into disrepair after the First World War as a generation of under-gardeners perished in the muddy fields of France, and many country houses were requisitioned for troops in the Second World War. But Rockingham's extraordinary Elephant Hedge survived, a remarkable icon of an eternal, unchanging Britain.

3. Pleachers and Billhooks
The Ancient Art of Hedgelaying

The hedger soaked wi' the dull weather chops
On at his toils which scarcely keeps him warm
And every stroke he takes large swarms of drops
Patter about him like an April storm

Each hedge is loaded thick wi' green
And where the hedger late hath been
Tender shoots begin to grow
From the mossy stumps below
THE SHEPHERD'S CALENDAR, JOHN CLARE

On a windy afternoon in March, John Treanor is laying a new hedge at Shepherd Meadows, a nature conservation site on the River Blackwater in Berkshire. He is a member of Hedge and Woodland Conservationists, a group of enthusiasts who meet regularly through the season* to coppice woodland and lay hedges. I am meeting him to find out more about the ancient art of hedgelaying.

These meadows were poor agricultural land, historically used as pasture, and a haunt of criminals, including an

---

* The season lasts from October to March – outside of these months there is a danger of disturbing nesting birds and trampling new plant growth.

eighteenth-century vicar who apparently moonlighted as a highwayman. Two decades ago, a shopping centre called The Meadows was built on the other side of the road from the river. As part of the deal, the developers agreed to plant trees for a hedgerow to screen the meadows.

The resulting row of hawthorn trees is now over head-height, and tall enough to be successfully laid. John is working with an axe and a billhook, the traditional curved cutting tool. (As a traditionalist he prefers not to use a chainsaw, though it is of course an invaluable tool for professional agricultural hedge-layers.) He makes his own hurdles and tools, and as a result they have a reassuringly old-fashioned feel. Today he is using his second best billhook – the best one has its handle broken.

Billhooks have been in use since the Iron Age at least. Richard Jefferies once wrote:

The billhook is the national weapon of the English labourer. As the lance to the ancient knight, the rapier to the cavalier, the bowie to the backwoodsman, so the billhook to the man of the hedges.

(In times of war longer handles or spikes were added to make them into weapons.)*

At the start of the hedgelaying process the row of trees looks nothing like a hedge; it is just an uneven line of trees and brush of varying sizes.

---

* *Bill* means 'knife' or 'axe', and this may have been combined with an ancient word for hedge – *haga, hag* or *hecke* – to make a word meaning 'hedge-axe' or 'hedge-knife'.

The first task is to select the trees that are most suitable for laying and remove any other trees and shrubs. This results in a large amount of loose branches and brushwood which needs to be left tidily for later disposal. (This 'lop and top' or spray would traditionally have been used for firewood and other domestic or agricultural purposes.)

Then John cuts unnecessary branches from each chosen tree and uses first the axe, and then the billhook, to chop part of the way through the base of the trunk. The trick here is to cut precisely, just far enough into the tree to allow it to be laid horizontally, but to leave the bark, some cambium (the layer immediately beneath the bark) and a little sapwood (the living cells that surround the heartwood) so that the horizontal part of the tree will survive the process.

This process is 'plashing' or 'pleaching'. The tree that is cut and laid is called the 'pleacher' and it is the basic building block of the hedge. Plashing leaves the tree alive, so that there will be new vertical growth from it.

John drives vertical stakes into the ground, and tucks the pleachers tightly together. They are woven through the stakes to create a solid barrier. The final stage is to bind the top of the hedge horizontally using rods in a repeating pattern, one under, then two over, woven together and tucked under for strength – the effect is somewhat like the woven strands of a handmade basket. The horizontal binders need to be flexible rods such as hazel or willow.*

---

* The old word for the osiers or hazelrods used for the binding is *eddering* (or *evering* or *heathering*). Fitzherbert's *Book of Husbandry*, 1534, advises that 'whan thou haste made thy hedge, and eddered it well, than take thy mall agayne, and dryue downe thy edderinges.'

The art of hedgelaying

John's second best billhook.

Cutting a pleacher with the axe.

The cut pleacher.

The line of trees is gradually laid into the hedge …

... with a few hedgerow trees left standing.

The horizontal trees are woven into the stakes ...

... and the binders stabilise the hedge.

The final result.

When a hedge is complete, the laid pleachers will immediately be effective as a barrier. Over time they will also protect the new shoots that grow from the pleacher (which could otherwise be damaged by farm animals eating the hedge) so the plants will develop from the original tight pattern into a wilder hedgerow. Regular trimming should keep the hedge in good shape for fifteen, twenty-five or even fifty years, although eventually it will become ragged and uneven and need laying once again.

A skilled hedgelayer at work is a really impressive sight – in a few short hours a line of ragged, wild trees is converted into a tightly packed hedge, woven in intricate patterns, reminiscent of Celtic wickerwork style devices.

In the countryside you can identify hedges that have been laid (and have a guess at how long ago they were laid) by inspecting the laid pleachers at the base of the hedge. Where there are horizontal (or diagonal) pleachers clearly evident, you are looking at a hedge that has been laid at least once. And over time the pleachers start to look more disorderly as the new vertical growth gradually envelops and distorts them, so the more orderly the pleachers and binders are, and the more they dominate the hedgerow, the more recently it was laid. Hedges that have been relaid over time can become increasingly complex – in his book *Wildwood* Roger Deakin describes them as 'works of the hedgers' art: a kind of tree jazz, improvised down the generations'.

Eventually, untended hedges will grow out and turn into *relict hedges*, gappy rows of trees. Even then, you can identify the horizontal branches of old pleachers and see that this was once a hedge.

Diagonal pleachers in a laid hedge, after a year of regrowth.

Regional Styles of Hedgemaking

John has been using the South of England style of hedge-laying. This is one of many variations in regional styles of hedgelaying – across the British Isles over thirty distinct styles are used. Different techniques are partly a matter of local tradition, but there are often specific historical reasons why they developed.

From the early days of agriculture hedges needed to be effective as barriers to keep wild animals out as well as livestock in. Coppicing and pollarding can create a dense, manageable barrier, and these techniques (or simple trimming) suffice for hedges around fields of arable crops, or for hedges around a garden or orchard. However, the 'weaving' effect of hedgelaying tends to create the most durable barrier

67

to livestock, so laid hedges have often been used for fields that contain animals.

Hedges that need to be cattle-proof must be taller and stronger than those built to contain sheep, while sheep fences need to be dense at ground level to prevent the sheep from wriggling through. Laid hedges can be single or double brushed (meaning that the twiggy ends of the pleachers are left exposed on one or both sides), depending on whether they need to contain livestock on one or both sides. If the hedge is adjacent to a road or an arable field, a single-sided hedge can be sufficient.

On the blasted uplands and moors, early barriers tended to be banks, stone walls, stockades and ditches rather than hedges, which couldn't be easily grown. Hedge trees on windy exposed ground such as the moors of Devon and Cornwall tend to have relatively stunted growth (though there are some larger hedges in the area, with one notable example being the famous beech hedges of Exmoor). This is one reason why the local style of agriculture used stone covered banks, which sometimes had low hedges planted on top. A similar style of turf bank was a common historical agricultural barrier in Ireland, where the bank was referred to as a 'ditch'.

In general, windy areas favour hedges that are broad and low rather than high and thin, while areas with a great deal of snow in the winter favour hedges with rounded tops, so that less snow settles on them. Rainfall levels are also important – in dry areas the cut pleachers need to be exposed to the rain in order to ensure enough water reaches them. Meanwhile, in some of the Welsh styles, pleachers are concealed inside the final hedge – the higher rainfall means they will still produce new growth.

Local styles of hedgemaking were also affected by the kind of material that was available, with some areas using coppiced wood (as the earliest farmers would have done) while others developed styles using machine-cut stakes or even rails. Other variations derived from the plants or crops that were commonly grown. In Lincolnshire the rich soil encouraged a wide variety of arable crops, and low, coppiced, thorny hedges were widespread, while in Kent, hop fields were traditionally protected from the wind by high hedges made from dense, unlaid rows of tree species such as pine or black Italian poplar.

Midland style

This is the most common hedgelaying style throughout the country, designed to be stock-proof on one side only. With interwoven hazel binders (resembling a twisted rope*) at about four to five feet from the ground, the hedge is bushy on one side, as the pleachers are slightly angled into the field, but relatively bare on the other side, which will often be adjacent to a path or road or to a crop-growing field. The prickly stems are on the stock-proof side and will prevent the livestock from eating the hedge. The pleachers are laid at about 30 degrees to the horizontal. This is a sturdy style, four to five feet tall, capable of resisting a hefty bullock (it is also known as Midland Bullock style) – it was traditionally used in areas of good grazing land, with many fields used for pasture.

---

* One hedgelayer I spoke to mentioned that the twisted rope style was usually bound as tightly as possible in order to prevent the hazel binders being repurposed by gypsies for clothes pegs.

Midland style hedge showing hazel binding.

Derbyshire style

This is a variation on the Midland style, using machine-cut stakes that were easier to come by than coppiced wood in the area. Hazel doesn't grow well in the relatively poor soil of this area as it prefers a lime soil. Once machinery could be used, stakes were preferred for this reason. In the Derbyshire style, binders are not used, and a narrower hedge is produced as the pleachers are not angled into the field.

South of England style

This is most commonly used as a sheep hedge, so the binders are used at a lower height, about three to four feet from the ground, although the style can be adapted to create a cattle-proof hedge. It is stock-proof on both sides, and the pleachers are laid at an angle close to horizontal to make the hedge secure at ground level. It is often used adjacent to a ditch, so the hedgers leave a short section of the stakes exposed, to give themselves something to hold on to when clambering in and out.

Yorkshire style

This style of hedge is notable for being shaped around timber railing, with a horizontal rail nailed to the vertical stakes. Sawn timber was originally used because stakes and binders were in short supply in the area – but a hedge shaped by

Yorkshire style hedge with timber railings.

timber was still more cost-effective and sturdy than building a fence. The end product is a low narrow hedge, stock-proof on both sides, generally used to contain sheep. The local field rotation system included a large proportion of arable crops, so a newly laid hedge could be allowed two or three years' growth before it was exposed to sheep.

Lancashire and Westmorland style

This is a rugged, practical hedge, that dispenses with binders, instead using a row of stakes staggered on either side to keep the hedge in shape. It is stock-proof on both sides, relatively quick to lay and very effective. The result, cut to a square shape, makes for a less compact and attractive hedge than the more complex styles.

Brecon style

Usually found on a low bank, this is a dense hedge that is especially effective for containing sheep. The stakes are driven in at an angle rather than vertically, meaning that they are close to being at right angles with the pleachers. Binders are used to secure the hedge. In addition to the new growth of living stems, dead wood is coppiced from the hedgerow trees and woven into the hedge to provide extra strength.

Montgomery style

This is a double brushed style using angled stakes. But unlike the Brecon style, the Montgomery style doesn't use binders – instead the top of the hedge is woven through the stakes to increase its stability – and dead wood isn't used to bolster the hedge.

Devon and Cornwall styles

In Devon and Cornwall an earth bank with or without vegetation is known as a 'hedge'. In the Devon style a low, dense
hedgerow is laid on the bank. It is secured with forked hazel
stakes (crooks) driven into the centre of the hedge to contain
the pleachers (which are locally referred to as steepers). The
laid hedge, which is self-binding, slightly overhangs the banks,
increasing its effectiveness as a livestock barrier. In the windier
areas, a traditional trick was to leave regular vertical trees with
one branch on each side which would be intertwined with
binders to make the whole hedge more solid.

Cornish hedges are stone-faced banks which need not have
any vegetation on top at all. However, many do have a low,
dense row of shrubs, which may or may not be laid. The base

Devon hedge, being laid.

of the banks was often formed from debris excavated from local tin mines. Making and repairing a Cornish hedge is a very particular craft, akin to building a dry stone wall, as it involves the assembling of the stones into a stable form. Today, the Guild of Cornish Hedgers is dedicated to preserving the very distinctive skills that are needed to maintain the hedges of Cornwall.

The hedges of the region also provide very particular habitats both for small birds, which nest in gaps in the stone facing for their homes, and for plants such as tutsan, which is rare in the rest of Britain.

North Somerset style

Somerset hedges are also often laid on banks, so there is a similarity between Devon-style hedges and those laid in the North Somerset style. This is another style that is stock-proof on both sides. Rather than using binders, flexible dead stems from the cut trees are used. These are run diagonally across the top of the hedge and tucked in to give this low, wide hedge a solid, impenetrable bulk.

Hedgelaying: Passing on a Tradition

Donato Cinicolo is a professional hedgelayer from St Albans. He has won the Hertfordshire hedgelaying championship five times, and now helps to organise the local competitions. His parents came from rural Italy and he didn't learn the art as a young man. Instead, having become a professional photographer, he went on a course run by the long-time hedgelayer Colin Wagstaff.

Donato with one of his prizewinning hedges.

Colin offered his students the chance to do unpaid work assisting him through the following hedgelaying season. Three took him up on the offer, but only Donato made it through the deepest winter months to the spring. Colin subsequently became ill, and he died the following summer. So there was a degree to which Donato felt that he was carrying forward a flame that had been passed on to him.

He gradually picked up work, from local landowners, the occasional farmer and the councils. He explains that, even where there are government grants, local funding for hedgelaying is often down to the whims of one or two individuals at the local council, so different councils have wildly differing policies. Many farmers simply can't afford the rates for hedgelaying, which is a labour-intensive process, so they continue to machine-cut hedges with a flail or else allow them to become unkempt. This is a particular problem where hedges are not currently needed as stock barriers – without the need to keep hedges stock-proof there is less motivation for keeping them in good shape. Unlike John Treanor, Donato uses a chainsaw for the sake of speed, but the traditional billhook and axe are still important tools for him.

His enthusiasm for his work is obvious. So I ask him to explain what it is about hedgelaying that appeals to him so strongly. First, he likes the idea of playing his part in a traditional craft. He admires a well-laid hedge in the same way that some might admire a fine work of art. It is fundamentally an anonymous art form – hedgelayers may be able to identify each other's styles, especially on newly laid hedges, but it is not an art that most people would recognise or appreciate.

Cotley Hunt hedgelaying competition,
Forde Abbey Estate, Dorset.

He explains that laying a hedge is a way of rejuvenating the plants in the hedge, thus helping the environment. A hawthorn tree, for instance, usually lives for 100–150 years. But if it is laid as a pleacher in a hedge, the new growth that results can mean that the plant lives for up to 300 years.

He is also fascinated by the local history that can be traced through an area's hedges. As an example, he shows me an earth bank crowned by intermittent trees in a local patch of woodland. A telltale sign that this was once a hedgerow is the beech tree – rather than one solid trunk, it is growing in a dense thicket of individual trunks, indicating that it has been coppiced sometime in the past. You can find this kind of remnant of old and even ancient hedges in the strangest of places, in towns, beside motorways, and at the backs of gardens – and the more you understand the signs of details such as coppicing, the more obvious these patterns become.

Through his hedgelaying Donato is helping to preserve an art that could easily dwindle or disappear. And, by training assistants and running local courses, he is helping to pass the craft on to the next generation.

Hedgelaying is an integral countryside craft that has lasted through the centuries. In the twentieth century woodland crafts went through a period of decline as farming became increasingly mechanised. It is down to a fairly small number of people that these crafts survived. For instance, in the Lake District in the 1970s there was only one skilled coppicer, Bill Hogarth, still working and passing on his skills. Today the apprenticeship scheme dedicated to his memory is one of many local schemes up and down the country which help to foster crafts such as hurdlemaking, coppicing and pollarding.

Beech stool on a bank, showing evidence of past coppicing.

Multiple trunks on sycamores,
indicating these were also coppiced.

If the art of hedgelaying does survive into the future, it will similarly be because of those people who are working to keep the craft alive in our time. Across the country there is a network of hedgelaying competitions and exhibitions organised by local groups affiliated to the National Hedgelaying Society. When I visit these competitions, what strikes me is that they are not just an opportunity for the best hedgelayers to compete and compare their skills. They also feature a range of beginner and intermediate categories, where amateurs and enthusiasts have a go at laying a hedge, and learn from the more experienced competitors.

Every competition organiser I have spoken to tells me that there has been a steady increase in interest and participation over recent years. It's well worth going to one, to see first-hand the enthusiasm with which the art of hedgelaying is being nurtured around the country today.

Hedgelaying, the next generation: Felix Pinney (aged 11) sharpens a stake, then hammers it into a newly laid Devon-style hedge.

4. Land of Ghosts
From the Wildwood to the Birth of Hedges

*Fields have meanings and memories for millions of us.
In their manifold forms, fields express our cultural
crafting of the land. They are our unwritten history,
carved clearings in the wild wood, the accumulation
of practical experimentation, invention and subtlety,
extending over generations.*

A MANIFESTO FOR FIELDS, ANGELA KING AND SUE CLIFFORD

We live in a land of ghosts. Remnants of the past surround us everywhere we go, in statues, old buildings, monuments and graveyards, in drovers' roads, sacred sites and ancient gathering places. The centres of our towns and villages often date back centuries, even if they have been built and rebuilt on the same patch of land. The soil is full of remnants of the past, fragments of old pottery, clothes pegs, scraps of cloth and paper and shards of glass.

Buried in the clay of my own garden there is rubble that probably dates back to the bomb that fell on the school field that lies beyond during the Second World War. Apparently school was called off for the morning, but the children returned in the afternoon once the all clear had been given. I recently buried a family cat in the garden, and found an unexplained paved layer about forty inches below the lawn – its age is impossible to guess, though it may be one explanation for the stunted growth of my miniature hedge.

History is an accumulation of the stories, ghosts and remnants that are all around us in the places where we live. Our first interest in history is localised. As children we want to know about our parents and grandparents 'when they were young'. And as we get older we start to become interested in the history of the places where we live.

In the lowlands of Britain we are surrounded by the last fragments of the wildwood. I grew up in an area that was once part of the Weald, and where I live now was part of the Middlesex Forest. In the countryside there are remnants of the ancient forest, in pockets of remaining woodland and in the woodland ghosts that still hedge some trackways and parishes. This is a country with many trees, but for every fully grown tree there are ten or even a hundred more that make up the hedges of Britain.

Our ancestors worshipped and venerated trees. Today we have cleared the forests and tamed many trees into hedges, orchards and managed woodland. But there are reminders of the wildwood all around us, and occasionally it is impossible not to notice them, and to wonder what life must have been like for our distant ancestors, before the age of the hedge.

The Growth of the Wildwood

I've come to Ivinghoe Beacon in Buckinghamshire, the hill where the Icknield Way and the Ridgeway meet. There was an Iron Age hill fort here, and for millennia before that,

The Icknield Way, on Ivinghoe Beacon.

travellers used the track that passed through this point. To the west it is known as the Ridgeway, and stretches down into Wessex, to Overton Hill near Avebury, while to the east, it is called the Icknield Way and leads to East Anglia, passing close to Bury St Edmunds and Thetford.

It's a July day, but it is overcast, with glowering grey clouds. A few kite flyers on the side of the hill are being battered into submission by gusts of bitingly cold wind. The Beacon commands wonderful views of the surrounding lowland, and the old trackways are clearly visible along the high ground, chalky paths leading back into antiquity.

At the summit I take a few moments to survey the land below, agricultural, hedged fields with pockets of woodland intersected by more recent roads and footpaths. A landscape historian could read information from the exposed ridges and dips in those fields, and see the traces of ancient settlements, ponds and ditches in the undulations.

A few thousand years ago, a solitary watcher on the hill would have seen a very different landscape. The valleys would have been densely wooded with the ground invisible beneath the foliage. Early travellers used these paths across the chalk uplands because they were safe thoroughfares, beyond the dangers of the forest. From this vantage point I can imagine this ancient scene. But the overall history of the landscape and its human inhabitants was one of constant flux.

Mankind's occupation of this part of the world can be traced back to one of prehistory's warmer spells 700,000 years ago, thanks to discoveries of flint tools and bones. At this time Britain and Ireland were a single promontory of Europe. The intrepid travellers who ventured out to this remote corner of the continent came along two main routes, over high rocky ground and alongside the beds of ancient rivers. Two of the largest rivers were the Thames, which flowed along a significantly different route, and the ancient watercourse now referred to as the Bytham River, which has since disappeared.

Early humans drifted in and out of the region in response to variations in the climate. *Homo sapiens* finally arrived about

30,000 years ago, at a stage when the landscape was mostly grassland and there were still mammoths and rhinos roaming around. The most recent period during which humans were absent was probably during the last ice age, which was at its coldest between 22,000 and 13,000 years ago.

The story of the modern landscape and our interaction with it really dates to the end of this ice age and the warmer period that followed. After the thaw, the landscape would at first have been tundra, with few trees or large plants. Large areas looked something like modern moorland, with a steady accretion of peat and bogs in wetter areas. At this stage Ireland, Britain and mainland Europe were still joined, with the area

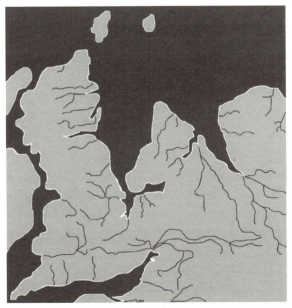

Map of the British Isles and Northern Europe in
approximately 7000 BC, showing Doggerland.

called Doggerland being part of the land that has since been lost beneath the North Sea. The sea finally cut Ireland off from Britain in about 7500 BC and Britain from Europe a millennium later. (The name of Doggerland survives in the modern shipping forecast: 'Cromarty, Forth, Tyne, Dogger, Fisher, German Bight …')

As humans started to spread north once more, the first to cross the 'land bridge' were probably hunters following the roaming herds of wild horses and reindeer, and perhaps traders searching for goods. As the climate became milder, hardy trees such as birch, aspen, pine and hazel gradually became re-established and spread, and the new wildwood started to grow. Other traditional species such as oak, elm, lime, holly and ash followed as the climate became milder and the wildwood spread. Since new species spread from Europe, from the south and the east, some of the slow-spreading species that reached England, including maple, hornbeam and lime, did not make it as far as Ireland.

The wildwood gradually covered a large proportion of the lowlands. So the least treacherous, and most easily navigable routes were across the high ground, especially in the winter – the Lower Icknield Way which ran along the clay at the base of the hills would often have become impassable in bad weather, just as the muddiest footpaths do to this day. The safest and most reliable routes into the British Isles were those along the edges of the Thames Valley, and along the rocky hills of the Chilterns, and the North and South Downs.

The growth of the wildwood also made life more complicated for the hunter-gatherers of the Mesolithic period. The herds of large mammals that had once roamed the country

The maze at Chatsworth House. (See pages 140–4.)

A remarkable avenue of 150 idiosyncratic yew topiaries can be seen on the estate of Clipsham Hall in Rutland. It was begun in 1870 by Amos Alexander, the forester on the estate.

House-shaped hedge topiary.

Different styles of billhook. (See page 62.)

A British landscape scene, with a recently laid hedge in the foreground.

Hedgelaying the modern way, with safety gear and a chainsaw.

A laid hedge at Prae Wood in Hertfordshire, showing one year's new growth (the vertical shoots).

New shoots growing from a pleacher a year after it was cut. (See page 63.)

*Poppies growing in a
hedgerow margin.*

Binding (or heathering) on a recently laid hedge. (See page 63.)

Hedgerow trees in winter.

Rockingham's Elephant Hedge. (See pages 56–60.)

A different kind of elephant hedge, a topiary cut by Gavin Hogg in his garden in Brecon.

became steadily less plentiful and harder to hunt in the dense forest. It took the development of genuine farming in the Neolithic period to give humans a more reliable source of food. And this development also led to the creation of the earliest hedges.

The Dawn of Woodcraft and the First Hedge

Neolithic agriculture spread across Europe from Africa and the Middle East from the sixth millennium BC onwards. The earliest British Neolithic remains date to about 4400 BC. The new farming techniques used a range of relatively sophisticated tools to tend, harvest and process crops. Tools of wood and stone such as sickle blades and grinding stones enabled the production and refinement of cereal crops. Ongoing crop production led to a more settled way of life, with communities staying in one place for longer. It became normal for people to live in settled groups that would turn into hamlets and even villages.

In the areas where Neolithic culture evolved there wasn't an extensive wildwood: agriculture started on southern plains, steppes and river deltas. But in Britain the Neolithic revolution was heavily reliant on the creation of fields through woodland clearance. For this purpose, tools such as polished stone axes and adzes (used to fashion wood into bowls, canoes and so on) were indispensable.

Woodland clearance is a monumental task, both back-breaking and dangerous. You need to cut or pull down larger trees, to dig out the stumps, and to continually grub out new saplings. In some areas of the world it is effective to burn woodland, but many British tree species are resistant to this method, especially those with broad trunks and thick, moist bark. So while some areas were cleared using slash and burn techniques (as suggested by place names such as Brentwood, Barnet and Burntwood), there would always have been intensive labour involved in clearing the land. The early Neolithic inhabitants had to win new fields and pastures yard by yard using limited manpower and without metal tools.

Along the way, they also became proficient at woodcraft and woodland management. And as they started to impose themselves on the wildwood, they discovered a hugely important fact. The new growth from trees that have been cut back is far more useful and flexible than mature wood. This is the secret behind the arts of coppicing and pollarding.

This dead tree stump shows the signs of past coppicing, in the many shoots growing from the same stool.

By managing woodland and rotating the coppicing over successive years, a constant supply of wood of specific sizes could be maintained. The shoots could be used for stakes, poles and hurdles, for firewood, and for other kinds of tools such as besom brooms, mallets and axe handles. And by weaving flexible, coppiced wood together, more complex structures could be produced, including wickerwork baskets and the large wattle screens and sheets that were used in wattle and daub buildings.

An example of the versatility of Neolithic woodcraft comes from the trackways that were preserved beneath peat in the Somerset Levels. The earliest that has been discovered, the Sweet Track, dates back to approximately 4000 BC – it was a complex structure made from poles of lime, elm, ash, oak, alder, hazel and holly. It provided a pathway across the treacherous marshy land that emerged above the levels in the summer,* and is the oldest known engineered road in the world.

The same skills that allowed Neolithic people to coppice wood were used in the creation of hedges. It is hard to create an effective hedge out of mature trees. The branches are too inflexible, and there is insufficient growth at ground level to provide a barrier. However, a row of coppiced (or heavily pruned) plants produces new, flexible growth at ground level. For plants of sufficient rigidity, this can be an effective agricultural barrier in itself.

This is the simplest form of hedgemaking, and was probably the most common live hedge for many centuries. In the areas of Britain least affected by Enclosure Acts, for instance

---

* I've always loved the old name for the Somerset Levels, which is the Summer Country – meaning 'the land that emerged from the water in the summer'.

A dead hedge made from brush.

parts of Essex and Herefordshire, hedges of this sort remain common today. It is also the basic principle behind most garden hedges, which are simply constructed from a tight row of plants that are kept to a restricted height.

There was one more major development to come in hedgemaking. At some point the most cunning of the early farmers found that by cutting a line of small trees most of the way through the stumps, while leaving the cut tree intact in a near horizontal position, they could create an immediate barrier that also stayed alive and grew. The new growth from the stumps could then be reinforced with stakes and poles to create a continuous, living barrier. This is the art we now refer to as hedgelaying.

It is also possible that some farmers or shepherds discovered the art of hedgemaking when they used coppiced wood to build a fence or 'dead hedge' and found that some of the wood took root, resulting in resilient new growth. And the dead hedges, fences and banks of early farmers would also have led to fencerows as live shrubs took root next to them and grew into living hedges. So it seems likely that there were at least some live hedges in use in Neolithic Britain.

Early Field Patterns

Of course the Neolithic revolution was no overnight sensation, and it took a long time for hedged fields and villages to replace the wildwood. The development of true husbandry of the land and permanent field systems was a long, slow process.

From about 2200 BC the Beaker people, who knew how to refine metal, started to use bronze rather than stone in most tools, making agriculture and woodland clearance a slightly easier task. We now have clear evidence of field systems dating to the Bronze Age – on southern Dartmoor there are parallel sets of long, low stony banks about 100 yards apart called 'reaves'. They are dissected at uneven intervals by cross-reaves. Archaeological digs have dated the field system to the Bronze Age, when the reaves separated fields that were used for arable crops and pasture. There are also reaves in Ireland –

---

* In *Hedges* by Pollard, Hooper and Moore, the authors assume that 'dead hedges', a commonly used medieval term, were fences, referring to the Penny Hedge traditionally built every year on Whitby beach to support this. This leads them to see the spread of live hedges as a post-medieval phenomenon, a view that I would disagree with.

and in County Mayo, field walls excavated from beneath bogs have been dated even earlier, to the Neolithic culture (which arrived in Ireland at about the same time as the rest of the British Isles).

Oliver Rackham (in *The History of the Countryside*) has suggested that some surviving field systems can be dated back to reaves. In the Saints in north-east Suffolk, there is a field system that replicates the slightly crooked parallel lines of the Dartmoor reaves. (You can trace this pattern using satellite images of Stone Street, the A144, which marks one of the longer reaves.) Here, he suggests, the modern hedges may follow Bronze Age patterns of reaves and cross-reaves, thus giving us a clue to history that could go back 5,000 years or more.

Cornwall is another rich location for early field systems. The layout of family farms with enclosed fields survived there with less disruption through the enclosures period, so there are hedges that can be dated back 4,000 or 5,000 years. One well-known example is at Zennor, in the Penwith peninsula, where the small fields, in irregular, nearly square shapes, have retained the same pattern since the Bronze Age.

Other evidence of early farming comes in the Celtic fields and lynchets that can be seen on large areas of downland and moorland, including the southern downs and the Yorkshire moors. Small, square ploughed fields were surrounded by banks. Where they were on slopes, the action of the plough moved soil downhill over time. Lynchets are the banks of earth at the bottom of such fields, against walls or hedges. They were either caused purely by the action of the plough or deliberately constructed to level the fields and make them more stable. Either way the result is a series of stepped terraces down the slope of the hill, which survive after the removal of the original field boundaries. In some cases you can observe ragged lines of trees and bushes on the edges of lynchets, indicating that a hedgerow was once maintained here, but was subsequently neglected. Excavations in some of these early fields have uncovered debris from the Bronze Age and even Neolithic fragments.

The next major breakthrough in farming technology came in about 750 BC with the start of the Iron Age. Iron is much harder than bronze, and iron axes were powerful tools for woodland clearance, while iron-tipped ploughs were far more effective at ploughing and cultivating land.

Population growth and woodland clearance accelerated through the Iron Age. By the time the Romans arrived large areas of the landscape had been cleared of woodland, including much of the South Downs, Salisbury Plain and the Yorkshire Wolds. Oliver Rackham describes this woodland clearance as being the greatest achievement of any of our ancestors.

Some elements of the resulting landscape would be recognisable to us today – there were small hamlets and villages, isolated farmsteads, enclosed pastures and orchards and large open fields of grain. A country that had been mostly woodland was starting to contain extensive agricultural areas and hedge-fringed fields.

Past and Present

In a historic place such as Ivinghoe Beacon it is easy to feel as though you have one foot in the past. But it is a feeling that can strike you anywhere. Visiting my cousins in Derbyshire,

I can walk across fields that were farmed by my own ancestors. Looking at the mountains of Wicklow and the green fields of Connemara I think of my wife's family who bred horses there until her great-grandparents emigrated to Manchester. As I walk the streets of London, I know there are old green lanes and meadows buried under the concrete and brick.

There are layers of ages in the soil beneath our feet – from the tundra of the ice age and the ancient wildwood, through to the more recent past. Contemplating the long sweep of history the whole idea of national identity starts to seem ever more complicated. We live on islands across which the sea rose and fell, while glaciers advanced and retreated, and the tide of plant, animal and human populations drifted in and out. Across the centuries, earlier inhabitants mingled and bred with successive waves of invaders and incomers, creating the complex, tangled picture we perceive today.

In the modern landscape with its hedges, boundaries, banks and mounds, we see the results of millennia of culture. Hedges were only one aspect of the transformation of the land, but in the clearance of forests and the transformation of the land-scape into an agricultural one, they played a major role. They imposed human design on the landscape itself, demarcating ownership rights, rights of way, pastures and fields. And it was the skills of woodcraft that developed as we tamed those forests that taught us how to make hedgerows in the first place.

Ghosts of woodland, ghosts of ancestors and lost tribes, ghosts of fields and rivers, ghosts of battlegrounds, trading routes and abandoned villages and settlements. When we learn to understand them, we come to know much more about who we are today.

The Giant's Hedge, Cornwall

Jack the Giant had nothing to do,
So he made a hedge from Lerryn to Looe.
OLD CORNISH RHYME

Around the British Isles there is a variety of natural or constructed features named the Giant's Chair, Giant's Cave, Giant's Foot, Giant's Punchbowl and so on. Much as I'd like to believe they indicate the ancient presence of giants in this land, they usually have perfectly good alternative explanations.

The Giant's Hedge in Cornwall is an earth bank that runs about ten miles from Lerryn to Looe. In Kilminorth Woods, where it runs alongside the West Looe river, it seems like a fairly normal hedge bank, topped with an array of woody species and flowers. However there are better preserved sections towards the Lerryn end, where the hedge is twice as tall as a man. The section in Willake Wood is still stone-faced with a ditch alongside it. Over the centuries there has been some erosion – two hundred years ago it was reportedly sixteen feet high and ten feet broad along most of its length.

The hedge was probably built between the sixth and eighth centuries to defend a local Cornish kingdom. One tradition has this as the kingdom of King Mark of the Tristram and Iseult legend; another relates that Jesus came here as a child, accompanied by his uncle, landing on Looe Island where the local piskies built a huge hedge to protect them. There is also a version of the rhyme that suggests the devil was the builder.

The truth is probably more prosaic. 'Jack', as mentioned in the traditional rhyme, is the old colloquial term for a Cornishman, and it is likely that it took the hard labour of many local men to build this huge fortification. There are remains of forts alongside the hedge. Woods have grown alongside many parts where there would once have been clear ground, patrolled by watchmen.

Whether it was built by the devil, the piskies, a giant, or ordinary mortals, the Giant's Hedge gives us an intriguing glimpse into the chaos of the dark ages. From 450 AD through to the ninth century, the Saxons (who became known as the 'English') gradually advanced from the east coast, making raids beyond their territory and expanding the area they controlled. There was extensive fighting between the English and the Cornish between 815 and 838 AD, but Cornwall was not fully conquered at the time. The last recorded Cornish king, Hywel,* died in 950 AD, and Cornwall was finally co-opted into the kingdom of Wessex in the mid-eleventh century.

As well as the Giant's Hedge there are two other huge hedgebanks in Cornwall that were probably created as defensive ramparts against English encroachment – Bolster Bank on the St Agnes headland and another Giant's Hedge across the Lelant–Longrock isthmus. Smaller defensive ramparts from the period were also constructed in the same way as a Cornish hedge – for instance at Chun Castle at Pendeen or

---

* Hywel's identity as a Cornish king is disputed – some scholars think he was Welsh.

Damelsa Castle at St Wenn. Throughout this period, when incursions from Saxon raiders were a constant danger, the people of Cornwall saw their hedges not just as an agricultural barrier, but also as one of their most effective forms of self-defence.

5. A Common Treasury for All
A Brief History of the Enclosures

Enclosures make fat beasts and lean poor people.
SIXTEENTH-CENTURY ANTI-ENCLOSURE PROVERB

Today, St George's Hill near Weybridge in Surrey is a place of considerable wealth. Tall hedges protect detached houses, with gardens of an acre or more, and there is an exclusive golf club offering 'Country Living at its best'. But in 1649, long before these houses were built, this was the scene of a famous protest against the 'enclosures' (meaning the process by which open common land was converted into private enclosed fields).

In the aftermath of the parliamentarians' victory in the English Civil War, the country was awash with radical ideas. In April that year local landowners asked Thomas Fairfax, commander of the New Model Army, to deal with a gang of dangerous troublemakers. Led by Gerrard Winstanley, the 'Diggers' had started to cultivate an area of common land on St George's Hill, digging up the soil and planting vegetables there.

This outrage was the last stand in their battle to protect open fields and common land from being converted into private land through the process of enclosure. They also called themselves the True Levellers, a name derived from earlier protests in which enclosure hedges were destroyed, or 'levelled'.* The Diggers were devoutly non-violent, but called for the removal of the hedges which were being planted around recently enclosed fields.

Winstanley was a fascinating figure, something between a mystic and a cult leader. He was a northern guildsman and bankrupt who took to heart the Protestant idea that the Bible should be a personal guide to life. (Early Protestant thinking was inspired by direct study of the Bible, which only became possible once translated editions were widely available.) He believed in the 'Norman Yoke', the idea that the land had been stolen from the common people of England in the Norman Conquest, creating the abomination of private property. He argued that no man had the right to buy or sell the land.

When the Diggers cultivated vacant and common land on St George's Hill, they were following his 'New Law of Righteousness', which aimed to:

Lay the foundation of making the earth a common treasury for all, both rich and poor, that everyone that is born in the land may be fed by the earth his mother that brought him forth, according to the reason that rules in the creation.

It is hard to believe that such a mild, religious group and their ramshackle little settlement of shacks and vegetable plots inspired such fear and loathing. But they were seen as genuinely

---

* In the sixteenth century the term 'leveller' referred to rural revolts, but by the 1640s it had been adopted by the political sect, the Levellers, so-called because they campaigned for greater political equality.

dangerous. The Civil War had encouraged ordinary people to expect fundamental change. Groups such as the Levellers, Ranters and Diggers were clamouring for far-reaching reforms, whereas the parliamentarians were mostly committed to the interests of landowners and wealthy merchants, who wouldn't accept radical attacks on the status quo.

Fairfax didn't want to intervene at St George's Hill. Instead, local landowners led by the lord of the manor hired thugs to systematically attack the Diggers. They suffered beatings and arson attacks throughout the summer. After a court case in which they were forbidden from defending themselves, they were ludicrously found guilty of being Ranters (even though Winstanley had specifically denounced the Ranters' sexual licentiousness and rejection of morality). They were forced to abandon their settlement and disperse.

The Diggers' stand at St George's Hill is still celebrated over three centuries later in poems and folk songs such as 'The World Turned Upside Down' by Leon Rosselson. But the occupation was a failure – a revolutionary moment had passed, and they were unable to stem the tide of enclosures.

The Enclosures – A Brief History

The enclosures first started long before the Diggers, in the thirteenth century. In many areas the open-field system was in use – peasants were able to farm their allotted strips of land and also to use common land and the 'waste' land for grazing, gathering wood and so on. The fields and the common land usually still belonged to the lord of the manor, but the commoners had rights of usage. Decisions about crops, harvests and ploughing were communal, involving both the commoners and the landlords, and most of the food produced was for consumption by those who grew it.

The feudal system was gradually evolving towards land-ownership as we understand it today. Lords and barons, granted land by the king, started to demand rent rather than labour from their tenants, and as the nobility won concessions from the monarchy, it became possible for individuals to build up larger estates. Inheritance by the eldest son (primogeniture) allowed these estates to survive and grow over generations.

The first wave of enclosures in this period came from two sources. In some cases, local grandees simply expanded their land by enclosing local wastes. In others a voluntary decision was made by villagers to exchange the open-field system for enclosed, privately owned plots around their homes.

Later, from the fifteenth century onwards, the growth of the wool industry created a major incentive for landlords to turn arable fields into grazing land. This marked the start of a more brutal phase of enclosure. Peasants lost their rights to use the land through rent hikes and evictions. For instance in 1494, sixty inhabitants of Bittesby, a village near Lutterworth, were evicted by the Earl of Shrewsbury to make room for sheep and cattle. The foundations of the lost village can still be seen in the ground there today.

The reign of Henry VIII (1509–47) was a turbulent period for the economy. Population growth and inflation, caused by Henry's high taxes and currency debasement, created powerful incentives for landowners to become more efficient, and enclosures accelerated as a result. Many believed that the enclosures were causing the economic problems (whereas the truth was that it was the other way round).

The fields were surrounded and subdivided by newly planted hedges, often of hawthorn and blackthorn, and these became the focus of popular anger. The sheep within the fields were also seen as symbols of oppression. The old prophecy 'Horne and Thorne shall make England forlorne' was taken to refer to the sheep and hedges that were taking over the landscape. Thomas More wrote a diatribe against these sheep in *Utopia:* 'Your shepe that were wont to be so meke and tame and so small eaters, now, as I hear say, be become so great devourers and so wylde that they eat up, and swallow downe the men themselves.'

Technically, enclosure required the consent of four-fifths of local landowners. However this was often achieved through a combination of bribery, fraud and bullying. Unsurprisingly, many commoners protested. In 1549, a wave of unrest spread across the country. In Kett's rebellion, thousands of Norfolk peasants attacked and destroyed hedges and fences around common land. A ragtag army briefly managed to capture Norwich (highly symbolic, as it was the centre of the English wool trade), and it took an army of 13,000 troops to defeat them.

In the same year there was a huge uprising in Cornwall, known as the Prayer Book Rebellion because it started in response to the new Edwardian prayer book. The rebels also opposed enclosures of ex-monastery land. The child king Edward VI issued a statement denouncing the fact that a 'great number of rude and ignorant people ... plucked down many hedges [and] disparked their parks'. Martial law was imposed with the instruction that no citizen was to 'pluck down any hedge, pale, fence, wall or any manner of enclosure'. Foreign mercenaries were brought in to crush the rebellion and 900 Cornishmen were executed. Many tenant farmers lost their rights to the land, becoming labourers working for English landlords.

In 1607 there was another huge uprising against the enclosures, the Midland Revolt. It was led by a tinker called John Reynolds, under the pseudonym of 'Captain Pouch'. He claimed to have authority not only from the king but also from God, and promised that the contents of a pouch he always carried would protect the protesters. At Newton, near Kettering, the 'most odious man in the county', Thomas Tresham, was enclosing common land. More than a thousand protesters attacked the hedges there, and the protest spread across the Midlands before the local militias regained control. Captain Pouch was hanged, and his miraculous pouch was found to contain no more than a 'piece of green cheese'.

Partly as a pragmatic response to the Midland Revolt, the government opposed enclosures during the next few decades. Charles I was quite active in removing illegal enclosures and fining those who carried them out. In fact it is arguable that this was one of the many causes of the Civil War, as the frustrated landowning and merchant classes were thus denied an opportunity to enrich themselves.

Idealists such as Gerrard Winstanley hoped that the parliamentarians' victory in the Civil War would lead to a more egalitarian society, but instead it led to an increase in the rate of enclosures. It has been said that once the monarchy lost its absolute power, Britain was run by a 'committee of land-lords' instead.

From the early eighteenth century, there was a final phase of the enclosures as new agricultural methods started to be introduced by pioneers such as 'Turnip' Townshend. Supporters of enclosure increasingly argued that modernisation was needed to increase food production – which was necessitated by the growing urban population. Of course there was some truth in this, but this was of little consolation to those who lost their rights or their land.

The first general Enclosure Act was in 1709. Between then and 1876, approximately five million acres of rural land was enclosed. Landowners could apply to parliament for an Enclosure Act, and if it was granted, the enclosure commissioners would arrive one day and draw up maps of how the land was to be redistributed. The main landowner received the largest portion (and usually the best quality land), but smaller plots were granted to each of the commoners in compensation for the loss of common rights.

The new owners were obliged by the commissioners to enclose their land, so hundreds of thousands of miles of new hedges were planted. So many plants were needed to create these hedges that there was a boom in plant nurseries in the Midlands. Hedges of this period tend to be straight, as they followed lines on a draughtsman's map, as opposed to the characteristic S-shaped curves of old ridge and furrow fields or the undulations of assart hedges. Since they were an obligation, many owners planted the cheapest hedge possible – as a result many enclosure hedges were flimsy single lines of plants. Today, a landscape of thin, straight hedges often indicates that the fields were originally laid out in the enclosures.

Some commoners established successful smallholdings on their land – but many struggled. Those who could not afford to hedge or fence their land were often forced to sell it to richer landowners, so the net result was a concentration of land into fewer hands. The dispossessed poor became labourers, emigrés or vagrants, or moved into the towns and cities to work in the new mills and factories. Many communities were destroyed by the enclosures.

Intermittent popular protests continued. Notably, in 1829 landowners near Oxford fenced in the marshy land at Otmoor and started drainage work. This had been common land, and local people were accustomed to using its resources. A popular rhyme castigated the Otmoor enclosers:

The fault is great in Man or Woman
Who steals the Goose from off a Common;
But who can plead that man's excuse
Who steals the Common from the Goose.

Regular disturbances followed and on 6 Sept 1830, a thousand people gathered and destroyed every fence and hedge around Otmoor. The enclosure was reinstated, but local anger and hedgebreaking continued for several years after the riots.

This wasn't just an English phenomenon: enclosures of common land and wastes in Wales caused protests such as those in 1809 in Llandeiniolen, and 1812 at Mynydd Bach, Ceredigion. In Ireland, secret societies such as the Oakboys, Rightboys and others destroyed fences and ditches in protest against the late eighteenth-century enclosures (created to service a growing export market in beef).

By concentrating land into fewer hands, the enclosures cemented the disparity between extremes of wealth and poverty that helped to shape modern Britain. The wealthy and powerful who had lived in castles in the Middle Ages now had their magnificent country houses, with grand gardens and a lifestyle to match. In 1876, a report called *The Return of Owners of Land* was submitted to parliament, covering all landowners who held more than one acre. At that point less than 40,000 families owned half of the land in the UK, while another ten million homeowners in the country held just 4 per cent of the land between them.

The balance of land ownership hasn't changed much today. Half of the land in Scotland, for instance, is owned by about six hundred landowners while the statistics for Britain as a whole have barely shifted since the 1876 report. The enclosure hedges of the eighteenth and nineteenth centuries still define large parts of our countryside, especially in a band running from Dorset and Wiltshire up to the East Midlands and Cambridgeshire. Landscape historians describe such areas as 'planned countryside', as the enclosures created a scene of larger villages, straight-edged fields and fewer roads as opposed to 'ancient countryside', which is typified by hamlets, winding country lanes in holloways,* and more woodland.

It is strange to reflect that these hedgerows, now seen as icons of rural beauty and preserved for their ecological

---

* A 'holloway' is a sunken lane between stone or earth banks.

diversity, were once widely hated for what they represented. The nineteenth-century rural poet John Clare was one of many who despised the new hedges – he compared them forlornly with the open-field scenery of his Northampton-shire childhood:

> *Unbounded freedom ruled the wandering scene*
> *Nor fence of ownership crept in between*
> *To hide the prospect of the following eye*
> *Its only bondage was the circling sky*

He went on to observe:

> *Inclosure came and trampled on the grave*
> *Of labour's rights and left the poor a slave*

6. A Green Maze
The Infinite Variety of the Garden Hedge

*Hedges, by the agreeableness of their Verdure, are of
the greatest Service in Gardens, to cover the walls that
inclose the Ground, to shut up and stop the sight in many
places, that the Extent of the garden be not discovered at
one View, and to correct and redress the Bevelings and
Elbows of Walls. They serve also to inclose and border the
Squares of Woods, to divide them from the other Parts of
the Garden, and to prevent their being entered but by
the Walks made for that purpose.*
THE THEORY AND PRACTICE OF GARDENING, A. LE BLOND

Compared to their agricultural cousins, the garden hedges
that carve up our urban and suburban landscape come
in a dizzying variety of shapes and species. While the country
hedgerow serves specific purposes, and often has to be sturdy
enough to resist livestock, the garden hedge can call on a far
wider palette of species. For instance, poisonous plants such
as laurel, privet and yew can't be used to protect livestock, but
are often used in gardens.*

---

* Although those with young children may also want to avoid such species,
especially those with poisonous berries.

It is the extraordinary variety of garden hedges that makes them so fascinating. Almost any species that grows to sufficient height can be made into a hedge of some sort. Within a short walk of my home I can find hedges grown from such different species as the unruly forsythia with its yellow spring blossoms, an acer with striking red star-like leaves, several distinct varieties of laurel, dog roses with their delicate summer perfume, as well as hydrangea, leylandii and fir. There's even a low lavender hedge, useless as a barrier or screen but with a beautiful scent at the right times of year.

There are two bamboo hedges, very different from each other – one is a wispy tall affair that sways in the breeze and is quite transparent, while the other is a dense screen, cropped just above head-height – I've never really approved of bamboo as a hedging plant, finding it slightly decadent or frivolous, but this is an example of a bamboo hedge that has been really nicely managed, presenting a slightly fluffy yet substantial surface to the passer-by.

A nearby *Lonicera nitida* (Wilson's honeysuckle) hedge reminds me of being an irritating child who loved stripping the leaves from a twig of this species between my fingers and throwing them aloft to turn them into raindrops. (I can see why this habit irritated my parents.)

Many of my local hedges are grown from the ubiquitous privet, box and yew. But they are cut in so many different ways that they have a fascination of their own. There are tall hedges, short hedges, dense hedges and flimsy hedges. There are square hedges, curved hedges, shaped hedges and down-right strange hedges.

Hedges in front gardens are particularly important in towns and cities. They bring colour to any street, all the more so when they are evergreen. Together with the gardens they conceal or reveal, they also allow householders to make a statement about themselves to the neighbourhood. Even if it was planted by a previous occupant, the way in which the hedge is currently cut and tended can give significant clues about what kind of person lives there.

I always find it amusing to walk the streets and try to guess what lies behind the front hedges.*

Hedge Psychology: What Does Yours Say About You?

This is a hardy design classic, the privet hedge with sharp lines and square corners. It is very practical, and can be attractive, though it is arguably the most conformist style of hedge you could find.

---

* When photographing hedges, a degree of caution is required. Recently in Gloucester I was confronted by an angry man with a dog. It was only when I showed him that my camera was full of pictures of hedges that he was persuaded I wasn't a bailiff or a burglar.

However, straight lines needn't be boring. Here the addition of a split-level design and a row of topiary square trees has added an element of fun to the mix.

This rather lovely effect has been achieved using mostly straight lines, but with a few angles and slants that give a more complex architectural feel to the ensemble.

Curves introduce a range of new options. The long sweep of these curves and the simple way the two hedges set each other off creates a calm, classy effect.

This is a more playful use of curves, with the undulating hedge suggesting an idiosyncratic, but orderly owner.

The curves of these closely planted trees create a humorous 'accordion' effect.

This rather serpentine effect is another pleasing use of curves.

Whereas this is really quite bizarre, reminiscent of crashing waves or sharks' teeth pointing out towards the road.

Some shaped hedges lie on the boundary of topiary. The first hedge above is cleverly cut to resemble a mantelpiece, while the marvellously exuberant second hedge reminds me of the weird cat bus from *My Neighbour Totoro*.

One of the classic hedge styles is the battlemented hedge, with walls, turrets and other fortifications. This could suggest a rather defensive individual, but I suspect that more often it is a sly take on the cliché about an Englishman's home being his castle. This is a modest example, but you occasionally see magnificent taller battlemented hedges which, in suburban streets, tend to suggest country house aspirations.

The battlement hedge is a refinement of the hedge gateway. A common suburban sight, it can sometimes have a slightly overblown air, as though it is trying too hard to hype the garden within. Hedge gateways are usually trained over metal or wooden frames, although occasionally you find examples where the gardener has been sufficiently skilled to forego the use of a frame.

At their most effective, hedge gateways (or even 'windows' cut into a hedge) can create a genuine feeling of passing into a different domain, or a secret world, thus creating an instant atmosphere.

Mixed hedges are another ambiguous signifier – in the 1970s there was an aspirational craze for 'mix and match' hedges, based on the perception that mixed hedges were often older and surrounded the posher houses of an area. However mixed hedges are often just a pragmatic solution to creating a hedge from scratch, as you can clip an existing row of disparate plants into a single hedge. So it's best not to be too quick to judge them too harshly.

The less common hedge plants such as bamboo, forsythia or fuchsia tend to suggest someone who really wants to be 'interesting' and different, but can still create a striking visual effect. I'll look at specific hedge species in more detail later, but it's worth noting that the choice of species can be as revealing as the way it is tended. Personally I prefer the old standards, such as privet, box, yew and beech, because they are solid and 'unflashy'.

The height of your hedge is as significant as its shape. Low hedges tend to suggest that you are approachable and open to the community – or alternatively that you are proud of your front garden or home and want to show it off. Whereas taller hedges suggest that you are hiding away from the world, whether from fear or reclusiveness.

They can also serve more snobbish purposes. Mature, longstanding hedges were traditionally associated with the richer parts of towns, so were a feature to aspire to. In her book *Estates*, Lynsey Hanley has written of how the middle-class owners of houses that backed onto her council estate in Birmingham would grow forty-foot fir hedges as a visual barrier between the two domains. That way they could avoid catching a glimpse of the estate, which they regarded as being of a lower caste.

Of course, tall hedges have also been the cause of many a dispute between neighbours – a subject we'll return to.

The Practical Garden Hedge

The psychology of hedges could fill a whole book of its own, but at this point I want to take a look at more practical issues involved in growing a garden hedge. The different species of garden hedge have attributes that address a wide variety of horticultural needs and desires. It is nigh on impossible to list every type of plant that can be used to create a garden hedge, or to give detailed advice on the cultivation of each species. Instead, I will focus on the functions that hedges serve in a garden, with examples of species that serve those purposes.

The fortress garden

When it comes to security and deterring intruders, whether they be animals (such as a neighbour's dogs) or human, there are certain species that provide relatively impenetrable barriers. The common agricultural species hawthorn and blackthorn are obvious candidates because of their spiky thorns. You do see hawthorn used reasonably often as a garden hedge. However blackthorn is problematic – it suckers prolifically, and without farm animals to graze on the young plants, it is liable to invade a garden and steal water from the soil.

Holly is another effective barrier – in particular hedgehog holly, with its sharper prickles. A hedge made completely of roses is feasible but it tends to lack the density that a true barrier hedge requires – however a mixed hedge containing roses or dog roses can be a formidable obstacle. An alternative strategy is to allow wild brambles to colonise a hedge. However, brambles are vigorous opponents that are capable of completely taking over a hedge. While autumn's blackberries may be an enticing reward for giving them a licence to grow, the security they provide probably doesn't justify the extra work.

A more ambitious option for a dense barrier is to hire a hedgelayer to make a properly laid hedge – several standard agricultural species, including beech and hawthorn, are suitable for this purpose. Species to avoid include elderberry or sycamore which can be laid but don't make good garden hedges because they overwhelm the plants around them.

Hawthorn.

Winter hedges and windbreaks

Many species of tree lose their leaves in the winter months. A bare hedge is not only unattractive, but also ineffectual as a barrier or windbreak. For these reasons, some of the most common garden hedge species in Britain are evergreens. Species such as yew, box and privet*bring much needed colour and cover to the barren winter garden.

Various types of cypress (including leylandii), fir, laurel and *Lonicera nitida* are also found regularly in garden hedges, while other evergreen varieties that can be trained as hedges include western red cedar, berberis, firethorn and holly. A hedge made of the evergreen *Viburnum tinus* will even produce flowers through much of the winter.

The other option for winter cover is a deciduous species that doesn't lose its leaves in the winter. Beech is popular for this reason – the leaves that start out such a fresh shade of green in the spring turn brown in the autumn, but survive the winter, only being replaced by new growth the following spring. One of the most beautiful, distinguished varieties of garden hedge is that made from the copper beech, with its gorgeous russet tones.

Hornbeam also retains its leaves in the winter months, albeit not as well as beech – however it is a possible substitute in areas where the soil is heavy and cold. Alder, which also flourishes in damp areas, does lose its leaves eventually, but not until well into December.

---

* 'Privet' sounds as if it should be related to the word 'private' but actually has a different etymology, deriving from 'primet' or 'primprint', which in turn are related to 'prime'.

Privet.

Yew.

Beech.

Box.

Laurel.

Hornbeam.

A well-kept, dense, but slightly permeable hedge actually makes a better windbreak than a fence or wall. This is because a hedge is not a solid barrier. It moderates the wind's power, but does not completely block the air movement. By contrast, a solid barrier such as a fence creates a vortex or low-pressure area on its lee side, so increasing the degree of turbulence. Of the evergreens, cherry laurel is one of the most effective windbreaks, because of its broad, substantial leaves. Various species of pine, cypress and fir can also be extremely effective in this role.

A splash of colour
While the practical side of hedging is important, some hedge plants are more decorative than the standard species. Hydrangeas can make effective low hedges while bringing the added benefit of their flowers to the garden. Forsythia is a flimsy, unkempt hedging plant, not effective as a windbreak or barrier, but it does bring a fine flush of yellow blossom in the spring, while fuchsia is similarly delicate but has those elegant blooms (which my daughter refers to as 'earring flowers'). Fuchsia hedges, also known as 'scarlet hedges', are a traditional sight in the Isle of Man and Cornwall.

For a low, ornamental hedge or border, various species of potentilla produce saucer-shaped flowers for much of the summer, while Mexican orange blossom produces sweet-smelling white flowers, both in spring and again in autumn if you are lucky.

Flowers aren't the only part of the plant that can contribute colour. Purple blaze plum has bright stems from which pink flowers grow in early spring. Dogwoods and scarlet willows

Hydrangea.

also have strongly coloured branches. Cotoneaster produces beautiful red berries in autumn, while pyracantha, which has white flowers in early summer, also produces coloured fruits later in the year.

Different colours of hedge foliage are also worth considering. Golden privets can be grown instead of the usual green varieties. *Senecio* 'Sunshine' (originally from New Zealand) is a hedge plant with lovely silver-grey leaves. There are various species of acer (maples) that have red or red-fringed leaves, while for a purpler shade, you can use species such as plum, pittosporum and berberis. Japanese spindle (*Euonymus japonicus*) is another plant with attractive variegated leaves, suitable for a low hedge.

Vita Sackville-West once wrote about a hedge in a small, ancient town near her that was constructed entirely from rambling roses. Always a writer with powerful opinions, she mentioned it mainly to lament the variety used, saying 'I hate, hate, hate *American Pillar* and her sweetly pink companion

[Dorothy] Perkins.' Instead she recommended using *Goldfinch, Félicité et Perpétue, Madame Plantier, Albertine* or *François Juranville.* I'm afraid I don't have such polarised views on rose varieties, but I do find her sense of moral certainty invigorating.

The scented garden

For a scented garden hedge, there are two possible strategies – either you can plant hedge species that have a pleasant fragrance of their own, or you can introduce climbing plants into a mixed hedge.

Escallonia* produces summer flowers that can be pink or red with a charming scent, especially after rain. Lavender can be used for low, ornamental hedges. *Eleagnus* x *ebbingei* is an evergreen that makes an elegant hedge but also produces wonderfully fragrant silvery flowers in autumn.

I always think that dog roses have the purest scent of all the roses, and they can be used either as a (flimsy) hedge on their own or as part of a mixed hedge. (In a previous home, I had a neighbour who was a bit too fond of his new chainsaw – one dreadful summer he cut down the holly bush and the dog rose that covered the fence between our gardens, as well as the fig tree in the front garden. Then, after that vandalistic series of interventions, he promptly left his wife and moved out, leaving our garden in a far sadder state than before he had arrived. It still makes me angry to think about the murderous sound of his chainsaw from the next garden.)

---

* As with other species mentioned, there are different varieties in the escallonia family. To avoid a litany of Latin genus names, I've tried to use the family name and refer to common characteristics wherever possible.

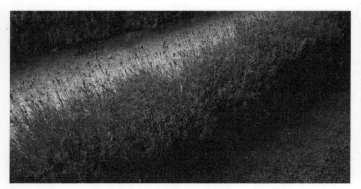

Lavender used as a border.

Sweet briar roses are also good hedging plants, with leaves that have an exquisite smell of apples when damp. Their hips feed birds in winter, and they have vicious thorns, making them an effective barrier as well as an attractive screen. They have to be kept fairly strictly pruned to keep them in check.

For climbing plants within a mixed hedge, as well as dog roses, you can consider a variety of species of jasmine, honeysuckle and clematis, all of which have the advantage of giving the hedge a hint of the beautifully overgrown rural hedgerow.

Beside the seaside
Seaside locations provide particular challenges, with salty soil and strong winds to deal with – some of the hardier common hedge species do prosper in coastal conditions, but there are a few less common plants that are especially well adapted to these conditions. Two examples of these are *Griselina littoralis* (a species that originally came from New Zealand) and escallonia. Buckthorn can also be trained as a hedge and is hardy in seaside conditions.

Tamarisk (also known as salt cedar) is originally from coastal areas of Europe and Asia and flourishes in salty soil. As a hedge it has a slightly exotic air – I've seen it growing most often in the balmier conditions of coastal Cornwall, Dorset and South Devon, where it complements the slightly Mediterranean range of plants that survive on the south coast. St Enodoc Church at Trebetherick in Cornwall is, remarkably, built partially on sand dunes, and is surrounded by tall tamarisk hedges.

High hedges

Where an imposing, tall hedge is not going to distress the neighbours, there are a few options for those who want one as a screen or visual feature. If you have the patience, the classic British high hedges would be beech or oak – but either of these can take generations to tend. One impressive example is the Meikleour Hedge, alongside the A93 between Perth and Blairgowrie, which is over 100 feet high at its tallest point and a third of a mile long. It was planted in 1745 by Robert Murray Nairne, who died along with many of the men who worked for him at the Battle of Culloden in the following year. Nairne's wife, Jean Mercer of Meikleour, gave orders for the newly planted beech hedge to be left to grow up to heaven in memory of her lost husband and friends.

Hedges can also be created from pine, although these are notoriously hard to maintain. In the Breckland, the area on the boundary of Norfolk and Suffolk, giant hedges of Scots pine, locally called Deal Rows, were planted a couple of centuries ago because pine flourishes in the arid climate: most have now been neglected and become rows of gnarled trees.

There are easier and quicker options – the much-despised leylandii has become widespread in this country largely because it grows so very fast. It also reaches extraordinary heights – the largest hedge in Britain is currently the double row of leylandii at the National Pinetum in Bedgebury, Kent, which at the time of writing is 130 feet tall. Other types of cypress and fir can also be shaped into effective high hedges. And while bamboo is a flimsy barrier, it grows extremely quickly. However it needs to be treated with great caution as it spreads rapidly and takes a lot of water from the soil around it.

Wildlife

One of the great things about garden hedges is the habitat they provide for wildlife, from butterflies, bees and other bugs through to birds, lizards and small mammals. Different hedge species are the natural habitat for different animals, but there are a few basic guidelines that can help to encourage garden wildlife.

A dense hedge will provide the most effective cover and camouflage, while the base of the hedge should be broad with some undergrowth of plants to provide food and shelter. The ideal wildlife hedge shape is a trapezium with the base wider than the peak. Good ground cover encourages small mammals and birds such as sparrows, wrens and robins, as it provides cover for them to forage in.

Most birds that naturally nest in trees will adapt to hedges. This is one of the reasons that tree-dwelling bird species have survived in Britain. Many original woodland species now rely on hedges for their habitat. Blackbirds, chaffinches, linnets, white-throats and yellowhammers aren't found in non-woodland areas without hedges. There are a few birds such as nightingales and tits that need a woodland environment for feeding as well as for shelter and roosting, so are rarely found in hedges. But many more species, including finches, thrushes, skylarks and jays can be found either nesting or feeding in hedges.

Birds prefer hedges that are overgrown and unkempt rather than heavily clipped ones – so while it may contradict other gardening imperatives, if you want to encourage birds it is worth neglecting your hedge to a degree.

Sparrows have been disappearing at an alarming rate from our towns and cities. One RSPB study suggested that the popularity of dense leylandii hedges was one of the culprits for this sad situation. These cheerful little native birds need a lot of insects in the summer – Will Peach, who led the study, said:

> The popularity of ornamental plants from other parts of the world, has made many gardens no-go areas for once common British birds. Many of the things we can do to help just mean being lazy, doing nothing and allowing the garden to be a bit scruffy.

He also suggested planting honeysuckle, hawthorn, wild roses and fruit trees to encourage sparrows in future.

Field mice, voles, shrews and newts can survive in hedges if they have the right conditions, and a broad base is again helpful. Frogs and toads will find refuge in the damp, leafy base of a hedge. For all of these animals, a mixed hedge using native species is the best encouragement – imported plants tend not to be natural habitats for the birds and mammals nor, more importantly, for the insects on which they feed. At their best, hedges are something of a smorgasbord for wildlife – they provide caterpillars for cuckoos, berries, haws, sloes and rose hips for a variety of bird species, earthworms for blackbirds, mice for owls, and small birds for birds of prey.

Hedgehogs, in spite of their name, do not necessarily need a hedge to live in, as they are fond of any area of covered undergrowth. However hedges do provide them with food and a route from one garden to the next. If you have solid fences and want to encourage hedgehogs, it is worth digging small holes beneath the fence to provide a passageway for hedgehogs who might otherwise find their way blocked.

Hedges have one more major environmental benefit. Especially when they are dense, they absorb fumes and purify the air around houses in towns, helping to counteract the effect of traffic. Their ecological contribution thus goes beyond the species of flora and fauna they help to foster.

Our urban spaces are becoming greener, even as the countryside loses some of its ancient characteristics. There are of course challenges for the future – for instance, it is possible that our towns and cities will have to adapt to an energy-saving future, in which suburban sprawl with car-dependent households becomes increasingly problematic. And the modern tendency to concrete over front gardens to create car-parking space is destroying many hedges (as well as making towns uglier and increasing flood risks). But throughout the country, garden hedges still have a valuable ecological role to play.

Hedge Care 101

It's impossible to give planting and pruning advice that would cover every garden hedge species, but there are a few broad rules to bear in mind.

Firstly, it is worth preparing the ground as well as possible. Back in 1821, in *A Treatise on Hedges and the Management of Hedgerow Timber*, Francis Blaikie wrote:

> There may be some difference in opinion as to the best method of planting and rearing ... hedges but I think there can be none in respect to the propriety of thoroughly cleaning and preparing the ground in the first instance ... the ground should be well loosened, fallowed for a year or two and have fresh earth or compost added; the better the ground is prepared, the sooner will the hedge arrive at maturity, and the longer will be its duration.

He was talking about agricultural hedges and it usually won't be practical to leave part of your garden fallow for so long, but in every other respect his advice is sound.

The other fundamental things to bear in mind when planting a hedge are the spacing and desired shape of the final hedge – it is easy to forget the degree to which plants will spread as they grow and to plant a hedge too close to other features. If you place the plants too close together, there will not be enough space for the plants to fill out into a full hedge.

When it comes to pruning, timing and frequency will depend on the desired purpose of the hedge – a wildlife hedge can obviously be more unkempt than a topiary hedge, while a hedge designed to provide privacy needs to be denser than an ornamental one. However, it is always advisable to prune often enough to encourage growth at the base of the hedge, in order to avoid a gappy or lollypopped hedge.

Hedges are also more likely to thrive if they have a slope or 'batter'. This means the base should be wider than the top, and the sides should slope slightly inward towards the peak. This allows more light and rainfall to reach the lower plants and branches and prevents the lower growth from being weak or dying out.

Good hedge.   Bad hedge.

Beyond these general guidelines, it's worth consulting proper gardening experts* when planning or caring for any hedge, in order to maximise the chances of success.

Growing a proper hedge always requires patience. This is true whether you are starting from small plants or waiting for larger ones to mesh together. This is easier advice for me to give than to listen to. When it comes to my own garden, I'm still waiting for my miniature hedge to grow into something

---

* In other words, not me.

that resembles the genuine article. Patience isn't my strongest virtue, and I've started to wonder whether to give up and use the box plants for an experiment with topiary instead.

My wife has suggested a row of ducklings would be appropriate. But she might just be humouring me.

The Chatsworth Maze

Like a nest of gardens, wall within wall,
hedge within hedge, more secret, more full of
fragrant and fertile life, the further you explore.
A GRIEF OBSERVED, C. S. LEWIS

Arriving at Chatsworth House feels like passing into another world. Noel Coward once wrote of such places: 'The Stately Homes of England, how beautiful they stand, To prove the upper classes have still the upper hand.' As if to prove the point, the fourth Duke of Devonshire famously had the original village of Edensor pulled down and relocated over the hill so it would not spoil the views from Chatsworth. The fact that *hoi polloi* are now allowed entrance to the grounds does suggest that we have moved on at least slightly from his time.

It is an impressive house but it is the garden that really astonishes. It is partly a testament to the wild inventiveness of nineteenth-century head gardener Joseph Paxton, who later designed the Crystal Palace. It was Paxton who created Chatsworth's gigantic rock garden, the gravity-fed Emperor fountain and the pinetum. A man of endless energy, he also built a coal tunnel, to bring fuel to the estate, and a huge glass-house in order to sustain a giant lily that had been imported from Guyana. Other notable features of the garden include the Cascade, with water falling across steps down the hill, and the weird willow tree fountain, from the branches of which water spouts miraculously.

I'm on the way back from a family wedding near Macclesfield – having driven across the windy Pennine tops, we head down through Buxton and Bakewell to Chatsworth. We make a slightly ragged arrival. I am hungover after the champagne of the night before, my wife is looking slightly pale and weary, while our daughter is dangerously overexcited.

Towards the end of our visit, we explore the maze, which was planted in the 1960s using over 1,200 individual yew trees. As our daughter bounces off around the next corner, we inevitably manage to take a different turn and lose her. We shout instructions to her over the high walls, but they just seem to take her gradually further away from us. It seems like a long time, but is probably only five minutes or so, before she is finally led back to us, looking somewhat chastened by the experience, by a kindly tourist from South Carolina.

Hedge mazes are an odd historical phenomenon. Labyrinths of various sorts were a traditional game, going back at least to Ancient Greek times. Myths and stories of early mazes (such as the labyrinth built to contain the Minotaur) suggest you could get lost in them, which is only possible in a maze with forking paths and multiple routes.* However European mazes of the early medieval period were mostly single path mazes. Like mandalas, which they resemble, these labyrinths had religious or mythological connotations. Cathedral mazes

---

* The well-known maze design known as the Cretan maze is a single path maze, which suggests it could not have been based on the Minotaur's maze, even though the two are often conflated.

were used as a substitute for the pilgrimage to Jerusalem. The Chartres maze is a good example of the Christian maze, with a single, complex route leading to the centre, symbolising the route to grace. Penitents would apparently wind their way along this long route on their hands and knees.

In the Middle Ages, mazes were often found on village greens and at fairs. Then, from the sixteenth century onwards, floral labyrinths and low mazes of dwarf shrubs became common in formal gardens. These early mazes still tended to follow a single path, like the earlier symbolic mazes, with amusements such as topiaries and statues placed along the route. As with the cathedral mazes, this technique created a long path within an enclosed area, but rather than being symbolic of a spiritual journey, it was a way of maximising the potential of a limited space and creating a playful element in the garden design. Finally the 'puzzle maze' with high hedges also developed, with multiple paths allowing the visitor to become lost. These more complex mazes became a part of the formal tradition, and persisted in British gardens for reasons of pure entertainment and befuddlement.

Today, there are plenty of mazes to choose from. Large-scale examples include the famous Hampton Court Maze, the giant maze at Longleat (one of several on the site), the Marlborough Maze at Blenheim Palace and the magnificent Leeds Castle maze, complete with underground grotto and exit tunnel. The Darwin Maze at Edinburgh Zoo, in the shape of a Galapagos turtle, and Newquay Zoo's dragon-shaped maze are perhaps best viewed from on high, while the maze in Dublin's Iveagh Gardens is a charming refuge from the bustle of the city.

The Serpentine Hedge at Chatsworth.

Hedge mazes are often made of yew and box, but there are examples made from species as diverse as *Thuja plicata*, leylandii and holly. At the National Centre for Alternative Technology in Powys there is an 'environmental maze' of rhododendron, birch and oak hedges, while Carnfunnock Amenity Park in County Antrim has a rare example of a hornbeam maze. (Hampton Court's maze was originally hornbeam, but has been replanted over the years with yew and holly.)

The Chatsworth maze is not an especially complex or epic design but it has all the elements of a classic maze, including hedges that reach over head height, crucial for that feeling of being properly bewildered. (I find low hedges, such as the two-foot box hedge in the white garden at Sissinghurst, less satisfying for this reason.) Hedge mazes work best when they are complex enough to create genuine uncertainty, and thus give a sense of real achievement when you find the centre, or the way out.

High hedges also create that slightly sensual, secret feeling in the very centre of the maze that makes you understand why they were historically used for trysts. (Although that was before the days when galumphing tourists appeared around every corner.)

Having escaped from the clutches of the maze we stumble across one final treat, the Serpentine Hedge. Constructed from two symmetrical hedges it undulates like a pair of sine waves for a few hundred yards, leading back towards the house. It is a beautifully simple ornament, planted in 1952, that gives the traditional avenue a humorous twist, and leads us gently swaying back towards the real world that lies beyond Chatsworth's gates.

7. The Hedges of Paradise
Formal and Sacred Gardens

We are a garden walled around,
Chosen and made peculiar ground;
A little spot enclosed by grace
Out of the world's wide wilderness.
'WE ARE A GARDEN WALLED AROUND', ISAAC WATTS

The well-tended garden hedge has deep historical roots. In early civilisations, the horticultural achievement that inspired most awe and admiration was the imposition of symmetrical patterns, formality or order on nature. In the oldest descriptions of gardens we find observers admiring the straight lines of plants or trees, or the geometric shapes of plantings in renowned gardens.

For instance, in early Middle Eastern gardens, symmetry was of great importance. In the Persian Chahar Bagh style (meaning 'Four Gardens' in Farsi), trees were planted in regular rows, and the overall layout followed a rectilinear pattern. The earliest known example was in the palace garden of Cyrus the Great at Pasargadae in the sixth century BC. In the same century, the Hanging Gardens of Babylon were raised above the city on arcades with formal terraces of trees and other plants. Contemporary accounts praise the orderly nature of these gardens and

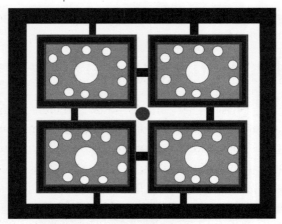

*A typical Chahar Bagh garden, quartered by channels
of water with a central fountain. Bridges cross the
channels and the 'islands' have symmetrical designs
of trees, shrubs and flowerbeds.*

those at Thebes and Syracuse, as well as the engineering brilliance that had gone into their construction.

In the following century the Greek writer Xenophon reported a visit by his contemporary Lysander to the gardens of Cyrus the Younger, at Sardis in Persia. Lysander was deeply impressed by the 'beauty of the trees, the regularity of their planting, the evenness of their rows and their making regular angles one to another'. And he was amazed to learn that Cyrus had planned the entire garden and could show him trees he had planted with his own hand.

When Homer describes the later gardens of Alcinous, he mentions the 'ordered vines in equal ranks' and the 'beauteous order' of the herb beds. In these accounts, we can see how the whole idea of beauty was closely associated with symmetry.

Where did this admiration for formality and order in gardens come from?

From Agriculture to Horticulture

In the first phase of agriculture, hunter gatherers learned to cultivate plants for food, medicine, shelter, clothing and so on. At this stage, rather than migrating to different hunting grounds, mankind started to stay in one place. Farming entailed 'putting down roots' in order to tend the same patch of land over a sustained period. So the animal urge for 'territory' started to turn into ideas of 'home', or even 'property'. In other words, mankind had taken its first tentative step towards the age of IKEA and *Property Ladder*.

For these early humans it was a major achievement simply to be able to cultivate plants for various uses. It took centuries of experimentation for people to learn basics such as collecting and planting seeds, harvesting, rotation of crops, the use of manure to avoid soil exhaustion and so on.

Early agriculture often took place within enclosures that were created from hedges, earth banks and ditches, or wooden palisades. The first hedges were used during the Neolithic period to enclose cereal crops. At this stage the barriers had a purely practical purpose, to protect the plants from predators and the elements.

Early farmers grew plants in straight lines, for obvious reasons. An even row makes weeding, cultivation and crop gathering easier, and you can keep track of your progress when dealing in rows. But it would have been rare for the patterns of early enclosures to become any more complex than parallel lines.

It was only when gardens went beyond utilitarian purposes to serve as places of leisure and contemplation that the patterns became more elaborate. In ornamental gardens, hedges play an integral role. They give shape to a garden, lead the eye and provide a backdrop for wilder plantings of flowering plants. And they can be used to create formal elements such as borders, labyrinths, knots and walkways.

There seems to be a general animal instinct to impose order on nature. Ants and bees build complex nests, beavers build their dams, birds their nests and so on. However, humans go beyond most animals in the levels of creativity they apply to this order. Give a child a bucket on the beach and they will build a sandcastle, give them a pack of cards and they will build a tower. But they will also go on to experiment with different ways of building, different ideas and forms. Most animals repeat the same forms over and over, but we get bored and try new experiments. It could be argued that it is this restless imagination that underlies our ability to use language, to make up stories and to visualise new inventions, from the wheel, to a house, to ever more complex horticultural designs.

Once people started to create decorative gardens, hedges and trees were cultivated for aesthetic reasons as well as for their practical value. And symmetrical or orderly patterns were important in these gardens simply because they demonstrated the owner's ability to impose themselves on nature.

Paradise and the Sacred Orchard

From our twenty-first-century perspective, it is perhaps difficult to understand how our distant ancestors perceived nature. We have learned to treat a walk in the countryside as an aesthetic experience, to admire nature and to enjoy an element of wildness in our gardens and parks. The word 'natural' is generally used positively, suggesting wholesome goodness, a lack of unnecessary human intervention.

But for many centuries, nature inspired a different kind of awe, one of fear and respect. In most countries, the wilderness was the home of predators, disease and danger (as it still is today in many parts of the world). In the Mediterranean and Middle East, it was a barren place without water and with few plants or food sources. In Northern Europe, folk tales told of the dangers of the forest, home to witches, demons and monsters of all sorts. The forest was a scary place, not a wood-land idyll.

Yet, at the same time there was widespread nature worship, and tree worship in particular. As well as being useful, trees were a symbol of growth and rebirth, and many cultures had myths based around the world tree, the tree of life, or wishing trees.*

There is a lot of evidence of early tree worship in the British Isles. The druids supposedly used sacred groves for their rituals and sacrifices. In *The White Goddess*, Robert Graves discusses the origins of the Irish Ogham alphabet (also known as the Celtic Tree Alphabet) and *Cad Goddeu* (*The Battle of the Trees*), a myth-based poem from the Book of Taliesin in

---

* The tradition of wishing trees still survives. Near Ardmaddy House in Argyll a hawthorn tree has its trunk and branches studded with hundreds of coins driven in as wishes; other examples include the old sycamore associated with St Fintan near Mountrath, County Laois, and the yew on what used to be an island in Eglinton Country Park.

which Gwydion brings the trees of the forest back to life as an army. Tree-related superstitions that survived into medieval times included the uses of green men in church carvings, rituals such as the 'Jack in the Green', maypoles and gospel oaks, and the protective role ascribed to yews in churchyards.

The cultivation of trees and orchards had devotional as well as practical aspects. We feared and venerated trees and nature but also wanted to bring them under control and cultivation. Many of the early gardens of the Mediterranean and Middle East were enclosed orchards, and in general early gardeners tended to focus on trees rather than flowers.

An orchard of sorts features in the stories of paradise shared by Judaism, Christianity and Islam. In Genesis, we see Adam placed in the Garden of Eden, where 'out of the ground made the Lord God to grow every tree that is pleasant to the sight, and good for food; the tree of life also in the midst of the garden, and the tree of knowledge of good and evil.' God put Adam in this garden to dress it and keep it, but when Eve and Adam ate the apple, they were cast out to the harsher land that brought forth only thorns and thistles, where Adam had to labour hard to cultivate the land. There is a similar garden reference even earlier, in the *Epic of Gilgamesh* in approximately 3000 BC:

> With crystal branches in the golden sands,
> In this immortal garden stands the Tree,
> With trunk of gold and beautiful to see.

The word 'paradise' is itself derived from the Old Persian word for garden – like the European word *haga*, it can refer to either the enclosed space or to the barriers surrounding it. (The fact that many ancient words for the enclosure and the enclosed space are identical is one reason why it is sometimes difficult to ascertain what kind of enclosure was being used in particular cultures.)

The original paradises were enclosed gardens (or hunting parks). Within, there was a lush, green area, with trees and plants, and water, whether in channels, ponds or fountains. The orchard of trees would be planted in a regular layout, while elaborate irrigation systems kept the trees alive in the arid climate.

Over time this style of garden design was formalised as an enclosed rectangle, with four channels of water dividing it into quarters.* In Islamic thought, the water represented the four rivers of paradise that flow to the four quarters of heaven, as described in the Koran.

The paradise style spread from Persia, Assyria and Egypt: first to the east, where the Mughal gardens of India are an example; and then to the west, via the Moorish occupation of Spain. The garden of Charlemagne was one of many created in medieval Europe. And in all these areas the word 'paradise' became a synonym for heaven. Used as a place of contemplation, the enclosed, quartered orchard garden came to symbolise the garden of God in Christian as well as Islamic tradition.

It was widely assumed that the Garden of Eden had been enclosed by walls or hedges, and this is how it was often

---

* Several are described in *The One Thousand and One Nights*: 'So they went forth to a flower-garden, wherein every sort of fruit was of kinds twain and its waters were flowing and its trees towering and its birds carolling.'

depicted in Christian art. However on a close reading there is nothing in Genesis that indicates Eden as being enclosed at all.

The biblical description refers to four diverging rivers, and of course the sacred trees of knowledge and life. When Adam and Eve are expelled, cherubim guard the eastern end of the garden, but no enclosure is mentioned.

So why was it so often depicted as an enclosed garden?

A believer might conjecture that paradise gardens were based on a distant folk memory of Eden, and that it had indeed been an enclosed orchard. The Hebrew word used in Genesis for garden (*gan*) is derived from the verb 'to enclose or defend', which could support this theory.*

As a sceptic, I'd be more inclined to suggest that whoever wrote the biblical text, in approximately 2000–1500 BC, referred to elements of the farming and gardening practices of their time, which included paradises. And when believers came to visually interpret the Bible they did so through the prism of their own times.

For medieval Christians the idea of a safe, fruitful refuge brought to mind their own experience, which included walled monastery gardens and, in Northern Europe in particular, hedged fields.† Many later gardens would also be explicitly based on the idea of a recreation of the garden paradise. The Oxford Physic Garden, created in 1621, lay within a square of

---

* *Gan* is also used in the *Song of Songs*, in a passage which can be translated as 'My sister, my spouse, is a garden enclosed, a fountain sealed up.' *Song of Songs*, 4:12

† Although what we now call a field or orchard was more often called a *close*, while *field* referred to open, unenclosed ground.

walls and was divided into quarters by two long straight walks, which met at the centre. Yew hedges originally surrounded the walks. Over the years there have also been numerous images of Eden that show it as hedged.

In Gustav Doré's Adam and Eve Cast Out of Paradise, *the angel barring the way back appears to be standing in a gap in a dense shrubbery or hedgerow.*

Of course, even if Eden was a real place, it is unlikely to have been enclosed by hedges. Hedges have always been most common in temperate regions with plenty of water. In these areas their flexibility and longevity give them advantages over fences and palisades, whereas in an arid climate it is wasteful to have a hedge that diverts water from the plants within the enclosure. The areas which have been suggested as the original Eden are in hot climates, suffering from droughts for significant parts of the year.

However, in the relationship between the paradise garden, early orchards and images of Eden, we can see how gardens came to be conceived of as orderly, sacred enclosures, in contrast to the insecurity and disorder of the world outside. And the formal, symmetrical patterns of those gardens helped to reinforce that sense of order.

In the gardens of the Middle Ages and beyond, people weren't primarily looking for a recreation of wild nature. Instead they were looking for something safer. And to this day the idea of a calm, ordered retreat within hedges or walls is a large part of what we look for in our gardens.

The Dying of the Light

Any time we try to impose order on a garden, or preserve order in one, we are engaged in a struggle with nature, which will constantly strive to return the garden to a state of chaos. Weeds grow back as fast as we can pull them up. Without constant monitoring and clipping, hedges and plants grow back into unruly shapes. We know that in the long run nature

Revenge of the hedge – this disused gateway to a house in Cheltenham has been completely colonised and filled in by the hedge that surrounds it.

can't be tamed, just as King Canute knew that the waves would not obey him.

Anyone who has been away from their garden for a few summer weeks knows how quickly it can become overgrown. Our primal fear of nature taking over was reflected in *The Day of the Triffids*, in which John Wyndham fantasised about a world in which the weeds had gained the whip hand over the humans.

If some unexpected disaster were to go even further and remove the entire human population of these islands, we know that nature would gradually take back its domain. Buildings would decay and fall. Roads would crack and new vegetation would grow through the tarmac. In the country-side, hedges would soon grow out, becoming lollypopped and gappy before turning into an unruly line of trees. The fields in between would be reclaimed by the wildwood.

Future investigators might identify the shapes of towns and buildings from the ruins and remnants of concrete and brick. Ridges and banks left in the soil would indicate the shape and position of farms in the countryside, just as today they show us where lost villages and Roman settlements once stood. But large parts of our civilisation would disappear without a trace.

If you take the long view, you can see the cultivation or preservation of a garden as an act of defiance against nature, as a kind of 'raging against the dying of the light'. In a way it is absurd to create such temporary works of art, but still we do so.

Perhaps this feeling of impermanence explains why there is a particular sorrow in those who grow too old to keep their gardens in the good order of their younger years. Sara Stein captures this apprehension nicely in *My Weeds*:

> There is no doubt whatsoever that I will be outlived by my garlic and that long after my own genes have been diluted beyond recognition, my bindweed's genes will be the same genes I left behind in my first, failed garden.

Of course some are lucky enough to have their creations preserved. One of the great surviving topiary gardens in Britain is Great Dixter in Sussex, where Christopher Lloyd, no fan of topiary, patiently tolerated and tended the rather bizarre topiary creations of his late father for many years. He wrote of the labour-intensive nature of maintaining the topiary, which dates to the early decades of the twentieth century. The annual clipping was mechanised after the Second World War, but while they aimed to complete this in August each year, it would more often than not take until November. As well as being an act of conservation you can see that this was done out of respect for his father. Christopher Lloyd died in 2006, but his legacy is now preserved by the Great Dixter Charitable Trust.

Rita Buchanan has written:

> [A shorn hedge] signifies vision, persistence, and patience – qualities we crave in today's world. Yet many people do make the commitment. They create hedges, care for them eagerly, and gain much satisfaction from the process. Why? Perhaps it's because shaping a hedge is the closest most of us will ever come to doing sculpture or erecting a monument, but I think the real reward is more mundane. Shearing is very empowering – it gives you an exhilarating sense of control and achievement. You can stand back afterward and say, *look what I've done.*

The religious overtones of formal gardening may have faded since the Middle Ages, but there is still a devotional aspect to the creation of a garden today. And any well-shaped hedge represents a minor achievement in the ongoing struggle between order and chaos.

The Secret Garden

*Empty gardens often seem to threaten an intruder, more
so even than the wildest country, because they are made
to be private. And who can tell whether, for instance,
a tunnel cut through a dense evergreen hedge will let
you through, or close in and catch you in the middle?
After all bushes are alive. They stand there and wait.*
CASTLE OF YEW, LUCY BOSTON

I won't reveal the name or location of this place, for reasons
that will become apparent.

On a cross-country trip I have taken a long detour. It has
led me down winding B-roads and narrow lanes that feel like
hedged tunnels. I've got lost twice and had to turn round in
a muddy farm lane to resolve an impasse with an oncoming
tractor. My destination is a country house with some fascinating topiary and a classic formal garden that is open to the public.

Except it isn't today. The door to the house is locked. No
amount of banging the knocker brings anyone to open it.

Hoping to at least catch a distant glimpse of the garden, I
walk past the house and down a lane that runs to the side of it.
After a couple of hundred yards, I leave the lane and scrabble
through the undergrowth, pushing branches out of my face,
trying to get closer. Eventually I reach the high garden wall.

Standing on a sturdy tree branch, I peer over the wall, but
bushes block the view. Without thinking, I pull myself up

on to the wall, and lower myself down on the far side via a pile of logs.

Now I'm in the garden, I sneak nervously through the bushes to an open patch of grass. Ahead of me is a solid hedge, with a doorway cut into it. Walking through, I find myself in a beautiful formal flower garden. Low box hedges create a geometric pattern, while the wildness of the flowers contrasts with the symmetry of the layout. There are tall fuchsias, waves of peonies and clouds of lobelia and phlox.

I walk along a wisteria-covered walk, pausing to photograph the box hedging and the surrounding hedge of yew. I would have enjoyed seeing this place under any conditions, but finding it in this way makes it all a bit more exciting. Like many, I read *The Secret Garden* as a child and fell under the spell of the idea of that doorway into a lost, fascinating refuge.

Through a second doorway, I find an area with knots and topiaries, beyond which a lawn leads up to the house. I cautiously edge across the lawn and start to photograph the strange, spiralling topiaries, kneeling down to get better angles.

At this point I hear a shout from behind me. Someone is walking rapidly from the house towards me. As I struggle to my feet, I've got a few seconds to decide whether I should run or stand my ground. The grown-up thing to do would be to walk over, apologise politely for the intrusion and try to explain about my long journey and subsequent disappointment.

Instead my nine-year-old self takes over, I panic and start sprinting back the way I came. Back through the formal garden, back through the hedge gateways I go. I scramble up and over the wall, twisting my ankle and falling over as I land.

I walk back through the trees and stand by the lane, sweating profusely, with scratches on my hands and a grazed knee.

I'm too embarrassed to walk in front of the house, in case I'm accosted, so I end up taking a 20-minute detour through the lanes round the back of the house, before trudging disconsolately to the car park.

Later on I examine the pictures on my camera. They're pretty poor, clearly taken in haste. The last one was taken by accident as I was running away and just shows a long diagonal motion blur of green and pink.

At this stage, I have plans to go back and visit as soon as possible. But thinking about it after a few days have passed, I'm starting to treasure the memory of discovering this place as my own secret garden and wondering whether a return visit would spoil the magic.

The more I think about it, the more I know that I can never go back again.

8. The Dawn of Topiary
Reshaping Nature

Our British gardeners, on the contrary, instead of
humouring nature, love to deviate from it as much as
possible. Our trees rise in cones, globes, and pyramids.
We see the marks of the scissars upon every plant and
bush. I do not know whether I am singular in my
opinion, but for my own part I would rather look upon
a tree in all its luxuriancy and diffusion of boughs and
branches, than when it is thus cut and trimmed into
a mathematical figure; and cannot but fancy that an
orchard in flower looks infinitely more delightful, than
all the little labyrinths of the most finished parterre.
JOSEPH ADDISON

No one knows who the first person was to get a gleam in their eye, take up some shears and chop a hedge or tree into the shape of a spiral, pagoda, cuboid or poodle. There is no patron saint of topiary, no revered founder of the cult.

Topiary is harder to track through history than agriculture. The shape and location of fields, hedgerows and earth banks give us clues about historic boundaries, cultivation and ownership. But centuries after a garden has been abandoned it isn't easy to identify which plants grew there, let alone how

Topiary can be practised on trees and shrubs on their own,
in a hedge, or in rows or other patterns.

they were clipped. So unless we have clear references in literature or art, topiary leaves no historical traces.

We do know that topiary was popular in Roman times, and Matius, a friend of the Emperor Augustus, was credited with its invention by Pliny the Elder. However, this should be treated with caution – the Romans often claimed ownership of ideas and styles that had been assimilated from other cultures and topiary may well have been brought to Rome by slaves or travellers.

There are some historical pointers to possible predecessors. Hieroglyphs suggest that the Ancient Egyptians may have been topiarists; formal Persian horticulture was a significant influence on Roman styles, as seen in the famous Gardens of Lucullus on the Pincian Hill; while the Ancient Greeks believed in the music of the spheres, the golden ratio and the beauty of pure mathematics, so they may have clipped greenery into geometrical forms. Roman gardening drew on all of these precedents, as well as others such as the Hittite and Assyrian cultures.

Whatever its true origins, topiary became a common feature in Roman ornamental gardens. In the first century BC, increasing numbers of wealthy Romans were choosing to live in villas in the countryside outside Rome. In periods of history when the countryside is dangerous, gardens tend to be walled, or concealed in secure areas such as forts or castles, and this doesn't encourage expansive ornamental gardening. Earlier Roman gardens had been enclosed in urban court-yards, or in compact rural enclosures where self-subsistence was the priority rather than decoration. But now conditions were more peaceful, and the new suburban villa gardens started to dispense with rigid enclosures, and to incorporate more decorative elements.*

The gardens of these villas were a mixture of open areas, covered arcades and courtyard gardens. They were laid out in geometrically precise patterns, with raised beds in which herbs and flowers could be tended. There were opportunities to view the landscape beyond, for instance through windows in the arcades. The Romans used a variety of garden orna-ments, including colonnades, fountains, grottoes, sundials,

---

* A similar stage was reached in British garden history when the landscape gardeners of the eighteenth century popularised the ha-ha, a ditch or disguised bank that allowed one to design a garden with uninterrupted views of the countryside beyond.

Statues recessed in a hedge, echoing an ancient Roman garden style.

mosaics, arbours and canals. Many statues of Greek origin were plundered, shipped to Rome, and ended up as garden features, a rueful journey from the sacred to the mundane.

Formal hedging was used in features such as labyrinths and the *xystus* (similar to what we would now call a parterre), in which geometrical box edging contained flowers or stones, creating a complex coloured pattern.

For their topiary, Roman gardeners used many of the same plants as we do today. One of their favourites was box, a plant which retains its shape well and is relatively slow growing, thus is good for edging as well as topiary. They also used cypress, juniper and rosemary.

Even with the slowest growing plants, topiary is an extremely labour-intensive art. The enormous amount of pruning and clipping involved was generally undertaken by slaves or servants, overseen by the chief gardener, who was known as the *topiarus*.*

Everything in the Roman garden became increasingly ornate in this period. The water features were major works of engineering, with shoots and fountains in ever more complex patterns – for example, at the Casa Nuova, or house of the Vettii, near Pompeii, excavations revealed a bronze boy, holding a goose from whose mouth the water spouted. To the modern eye it is somewhat reminiscent of an embarrassing 1970s plastic water feature.

It is worth quoting at length from one of Pliny the Younger's letters, in the first century AD, as it gives such a clear image of what the gardens of a villa pseudo-urbana looked like:

My villa is so advantageously situated, that it commands a full view of all the country round; yet you approach it by so insensible a rise, that you find yourself upon an eminence, without perceiving you ascended. Behind, but at a great distance, stand the Apennine mountains ... In the front of the portico is a sort of terrace, embellished with various figures, and bounded with a box hedge, from whence you descend by an easy slope, adorned with the representation of divers animals, in box, answering alternately to each other, into a lawn overspread with the soft – I had almost said the liquid – Acanthus: this is surrounded by a walk enclosed with tonsile ever-greens, shaped into a variety of forms.

---

* The title *topiarus* didn't imply that topiary was his only, or even main function at this point – the use of the term 'topiary' in its current sense came about later, in the Renaissance period.

He also describes an area bounded by clipped hedges:

> The box is cut into a thousand different forms, sometimes in
> letters expressing the name of the master, sometimes that of
> the artificer, whilst here and there little obelisks rise …

Topiary fashion became more preposterous as Roman grandees sought to outdo one another in the opulence of their
gardens. The historian H. Inigo Triggs reports that topiaries
were 'cut into pyramids, cones, and other geometrical forms
… figures of men and animals were often employed, and in
some cases a hunt or an entire fleet was represented in topiary.'

The increasing frivolity and tackiness of Roman topiary
and gardening could be seen as a minor symptom of the
decline of the Empire. Pliny the Younger was born in AD 61,
in the reign of Nero, between the emperor's brutal murder of
his mother and the fire that devastated the capital. When he
was writing self-congratulatory letters about his garden, the
poisoned seeds of Rome's fall into pampered decadence and
instability were already in the soil.

In modern Britain we might see a parallel for this decadence in the ornate, nouveau riche style associated with
footballers' WAGs and *Hello* magazine weddings. Amusingly,
the Manchester United player Gary Neville has created a
massive topiary MUFC badge outside his own villa pseudo-
urbana in the north-west. Perhaps the pattern formed by the
remnants of its roots will puzzle some future archaeologist,
like the feet of Ozymandias standing in the desert.

Romans in Britain

Julius Caesar's first expedition to Britain, during which he had to fight his way through those thorny hedges of the Belgic tribes of Gaul (see page 32), was in 55 BC. Whilst he made significant inroads into Britain, he was forced to take his army back to Gaul to put down rebellious locals. It was not until AD 43 that the Romans returned in force to Britain, during the reign of Claudius.

So in gardening terms, the Roman occupation came in the period when the villa pseudo-urbana back in Italy was approaching its most overblown. Excavations at Roman sites such as Coninbriga in Portugal and the palace at Fishbourne in Sussex indicate that many of the gardening fashions from home were recreated at the furthest reaches of the Roman Empire. This was probably the first time topiary came to the British Isles, though of course we can't be certain that the Celts or the Druids or earlier inhabitants of the British Isles didn't like to sculpt their greenery.

Under the Romans, southern England became peaceful enough for a large number of villas and a few palaces to be built in the countryside. Recently, the Fishbourne garden was reconstructed using a plan based on remnants of bedding trenches, tree pits and post holes that were preserved in the clay soil. It is a formal layout, with a wide central path dividing two symmetrical areas. The paths are lined with hedges, containing semi-circular recesses that would originally have been used to display flowers, statues or seats. A particular joy in the garden today is the intricately patterned box hedging.

Fishbourne was a high-status building, with a complex garden plan, but smaller Roman gardens have also been excavated. In the Roman town of Silchester, in the north of Hampshire, archaeologists have investigated a number of urban gardens, which were less elaborate, with many plants grown for use rather than decoration. There is evidence of cultivation of plants such as parsley, alexanders, cabbages, walnuts, vines and roses, the Madonna Lily, the sweet chestnut, quince, plum and apricot trees, all of which were introduced to Britain by the Romans and would survive their eventual departure.

The Romans transformed this country. To the astonishment of the indigenous inhabitants, they brought straight roads, advanced architecture and ornamental gardens to these shores for the first time. But the first flourishing of formal gardening and topiary in Britain was a relatively brief one in the long sweep of history.

By the start of the fifth century the power of the Romans was steadily declining, and through the first decade of that century there was a series of troop mutinies and Saxon raids on the east coast. Upon the final departure of the Romans in AD 410, parts of the country descended into local warfare. Some areas previously ruled by the Romans disintegrated into separate fiefdoms and the barbarian incursions gradually increased in scale and intensity, while other areas simply fell back into rural poverty.

Some vacated villas, farmsteads and towns were occupied by Britons, especially in peaceful areas. But the formal gardens in town and country would quickly have fallen into disrepair as subsistence gardening took priority over ornamentation.

Eventually the remaining settlements and buildings were abandoned, either because they started to crumble or because they were in exposed positions in dangerous times. As weeds sprung up and the seeds of trees were blown in on the wind, gardens that had once been the height of cultured beauty gradually disappeared into the undergrowth or fell back under the wildwood.

As the dark ages descended, the art of horticulture would only be preserved in any real sense in the Anglo-Saxon period behind the walls of the monasteries.

Topiary Today

After this first brief flowering, topiary was absent from Britain for centuries. It would only come back into vogue in the Renaissance period, when we started to hark back to the Roman Empire as a golden age of culture and order, and to mimic classical styles in architecture, horticulture and other arts.

To the Renaissance gardener, the formality and structure of topiary was a signifier of high culture. And while the popularity of topiary has varied in the intervening centuries, it has survived to become a gloriously strange part of our gardening culture today.

The basic techniques used by the modern topiarist are much the same as those used by the Romans: training plants to grow in the right directions and forms by using frames or suitable ties, laboriously clipping the plant with or without templates, and cutting at the right times of the year to inflict minimum damage.

If you are hankering to create a topiary hedge, the best bet is to go for plants that grow slowly, and that retain a fairly rigid

The topiaries of Cliveden include a songbird wearing deelyboppers and a primitive helter-skelter. When contemplating the hard work and ingenuity that has gone into such elaborate topiary, the first question that comes to mind is: why?

171

shape. Topiary specialist James Crebbin Bailey recommends box, yew, phillyrea latifolia and bay. Alternatives include holly, beech, rosemary, hawthorn, privet, juniper and hornbeam, all of which retain their shape well after clipping.

Some of the most elaborate modern topiaries are made by using wicker or wire frames, lined with turf. The incredible topiaries of the film *Edward Scissorhands* were, for instance, created this way. But this is a technique that the topiary purist would dismiss as a bit of a quick fix or a cheat.

Traditional topiary is an art that requires great patience. For instance, Anthony Blagg, curator of the topiary website Frost at Midnight,* moved into his current home in 1990 and started clipping the trees in his garden into shape. Over the past two decades he has continued to develop and tend these green sculptures, and even now he sees them as a work in progress.

His own topiaries are cut from yew and box, the perennial favourite topiary plants. The practical pleasure of creating them has gradually led him on to a more academic interest in the history of topiary. For instance, he tells me that Queen Anne had all the box removed from Hampton Court because she hated its odour – it can be an odd, sour smell, but even for a Stuart monarch this seems a bit fussy.

The long-term commitment required to create topiary can border on obsession. Many pieces take years to reach their full shape, and you need a great deal of patience to take a plant and create a sculpture from it. This is one reason why topiary tends to come in and out of fashion in fairly definite

---

* The name comes from a Coleridge poem, and relates to the fact that topiary gives a garden form and beauty even in the depths of winter. The site includes a useful guide to Britain's finest topiary gardens.

Cat or owl?

waves – some garden styles persist over time even if they are left untended, but if you stop caring for a topiary it will soon grow out. So it is all the more remarkable that this country contains so many notable topiary gardens that date back one, two, even three centuries, including the marvels of Elvaston, Chirk Castle in Clywd and Drummond Castle.

And topiary is not restricted to country houses or grand gardens. Some of the most whimsical topiaries of recent decades have been grown on humble garden hedges. There was a particular boom in suburban topiary in the austere post-war years, when it was a way of creating something spectacular in a garden, without great expense. Some extraordinary examples have been allowed to grow out over the years – Anthony Blagg told me about a splendid Loch Ness monster in Quinton in Birmingham that is sadly no longer there. But there are still occasional topiary treats to be found on the streets of British towns and villages.

There is always a moment of humorous incongruity when you come across a topiary cat, ship or face amongst the symmetrical hedges of a perfectly ordinary back street.

Levens Hall

Of all formal things in the world, a clipped hedge is the most formal; and of all the informal things in the world, a forest tree is the most informal.
HENRY WARD BEECHER

Driving north from Manchester up the M6, I'm not surprised to hit a wall of drizzle as I approach the lower end of the Lake District. West of the Pennines, rain is rarely in short supply. I'm cheerfully reminded of the two actors in *Withnail and I* driving away to go 'on holiday by accident'. I always enjoy being in this part of the country; my mother used to live in the lovely Eden Valley, between the lakes and the Pennines, not far from the imposing silhouette of Cross Fell, the peak of which was often lost in the low clouds when I visited.

About twenty miles south of Kendal, the sun manages to struggle through the clouds and a perfect rainbow appears ahead of me. The end of the rainbow points close to my destination, which seems appropriate given the wonders I am on my way towards.

Levens Hall is a mecca for British topiary enthusiasts. It's one of the weirdest, most astonishing topiary gardens in the world. I haven't visited for years, but it has changed very little since I was last here. As soon as I walk through the garden gates the same sense of being in a surrealist illustration or fantasy place, somewhere outside the normal world altogether, comes back to me.

There has been a dwelling here since the thirteenth century, when the de Redman family built a pele tower (a fortified keep). In the 1590s it became the largest house in this part of the country when the Bellingham family, who were wealthy landowners, incorporated the tower into a larger residence. Local craftsmen made the stained glass and carved oak panelling, and created elaborate plasterwork in an Italian style which includes Elizabeth the First's coat of arms and can still be seen today. In 1688 Colonel James Grahme won the house playing cards – he added external carvings including a heart, to represent the Ace of Hearts with which he won the decisive game.

It was Colonel Grahme who decided to create the topiary garden, and planned a set of extravagant, sprawling shaped hedges and trees. He was assisted by Guillaume Beaumont, a French gardener who had graduated from work at Versailles and Hampton Court.

The traditional Renaissance style was close to that visible today at many stately homes – regular shapes, boxes and cylinders, creating an orderly pattern. Levens Hall, where the topiary has been maintained to this day, is something far more astonishing. The greenery was cropped into a mass of strange discs and bridges, asymmetrical patterns and organic shapes. It was one of the most extraordinary topiary gardens in the country, but to the modern eye it seems to be simultaneously a celebration and a sly parody of the formal style.

For anyone who loves topiary or formal gardens, Levens Hall is unmissable. The glorious double beech hedges would be enough of an attraction on their own. They feature doorways leading from one section of the garden to another. On the way in you perceive the hedge as a blank surface of interlocking beech leaves. Walking through the doorway you discover another world, as you are in the middle of a double row of beeches, with ancient, gnarled, twisted branches, some of them held up by wooden props. It is like opening up an impassive piece of machinery and discovering the mechanism whirring away inside.

In addition to these hedges, there is a young willow labyrinth to the rear of the gardens, a fine circuit of pollarded limes around a fountain, a crenellated yew hedge from the late nineteenth century and a more recent hornbeam hedge. At one end of the garden there is a classic ha-ha, a hidden bank over a ditch, giving you unimpeded views of an oak avenue on the estate.

But the undoubted stars of the garden are the topiaries, which rise from a lake of flowers in a box-edged parterre. Once seen, they will never be forgotten. While the formal style went out of fashion across the country in later centuries, the gardeners of Levens Hall kept the faith, trimming the formal box edging, and preserving the visions of Grahme and Beaumont by maintaining, propping up and reclipping the yew trees in those peculiar, twisting shapes.

Chris Crowder has been head gardener here for nearly twenty-five years, and tells me he would be happy to stay another twenty-five. He is tending about thirty new topiaries in order to maintain the garden for the long term, but the spirit of the garden has remained unchanged. A few of the original holly and hornbeam specimens have died or been removed over the years, but a high proportion of the original topiary trees are over three hundred years old and still going strong.

Eventually, the vagaries of garden fashion brought Levens Hall back to wider attention in the Victorian period as an example of a style that was archaic at that stage. Many contemporary formal gardens had been destroyed in the landscape gardening mania. Levens Hall probably only escaped because it wasn't the main home of the owners, but was used as an occasional retreat or holiday home, so they didn't feel the need to update the garden style. It is this lucky chance, and the hard work of generations of gardeners, that means that we can still see it today.

As I leave Levens Hall, after a couple of hours of enjoyable meandering, I pass one of the other attractions, a half-size Traction Engine called 'Little Gem' – there is a collection of historic traction engines at the house. The sun has come out fully now, and it glints off the metal, showing up the bright carousel colours of the engine. Like a five-year-old, I wave to the driver, and he waves back. It makes me feel ridiculously happy, and rounds off a beautiful day.

Levens Hall.

Part Two
GROWTH AND CONSERVATION

Concerning the role hedges played in shaping and defining modern Britain

Preamble
A Modest Proposal

Inside the garden, we can construct a country of our
own. Several old trees, a considerable variety of level,
several well-grown hedges to divide our garden into
provinces ... Nothing is more delightful than a succession
of small lawns, opening one out of the other through tall
hedges; these have all the charm of the old bowling-green
repeated, do not require the labour of many trimmers,
and afford a series of changes.
ESSAYS OF TRAVEL, ROBERT LOUIS STEVENSON

I'd like to propose the hedgerow as the new national symbol of Britain: a green, gold and brown design to replace the red, white and blue of the Union Jack. It might sound a ridiculous suggestion, but bear with me while I explain.

I've always had a few problems with the Union Jack.* To start with it's actually quite ugly, and difficult to draw accurately to boot. I have never even known which way up to hang

---

* For any pedants or copy-editors who feel a bout of nitpicking about how
it is really called 'the Union Flag' coming over them, I'd observe that 'Union
Jack' is the most commonly used name for the flag, and the two have been used
interchangeably over the centuries.

it – the wrong way up and it signals SOS. Putting a stamp on an envelope with the Queen's head upside-down is supposedly an act of treason, so you can't be too careful.

The flag was originally an attempt to graphically express the unity of the separate nations of the United Kingdom under a single symbol. James I of England (aka James VI of Scotland) introduced it in 1606, shortly after the Union of the Crowns,* hoping to persuade the English and Scottish peoples to accept the idea of 'Britain'. Since Wales was at that time a part of England, it was not included in the design, which slapped the cross of St George on top of the cross of St Andrew in a rather provocative manner.

The design became even more intricate after the 1801 Acts of Union with Ireland when the St Patrick's cross was added to the mix. Unlike the English and Scottish symbols this diagonal red cross had not been widely used in Ireland – in fact it was a symbol of the Fitzgerald family, which had been a formidable part of the Anglo-Irish establishment since the arrival of their Norman ancestors.

So we ended up with a flag that represents confusion, stamps the English flag on top of two others, and ignores the Welsh altogether. Even the English component, the St George's cross, is rather odd, being named for a semi-mythical figure who was Turkish in origin and is claimed as patron saint by a panoply of countries including Portugal and Ethiopia.

Frankly, the Union Jack reminds me of nothing more than a garishly painted five-bar gate. It says nothing about

---

* The actual Act of Union didn't come until a century later, when Scotland had been economically weakened by the financial disaster of the Darien scheme.

The flag of St George, Patron Saint for Hire.

the Britain I know, a land of agriculture, declining industry, suburban towns, fields of wheat and heather-covered moors, cities with great extremes of wealth and dirt, and B-roads wandering through unknown villages.

I'd like a flag that encapsulates these aspects of Britain. When I visualise this country, the colour scheme I see is the green, gold, brown and black of a rural hedgerow, with perhaps the dazzling white flecks of the May hawthorn flowers. Our three main political parties already have a tree, a rose and a bird as their symbols. Why not carry this rustic imagery through into the national symbol?

I don't have a specific design in mind. Perhaps we could have a national competition to be judged by Alan Titchmarsh, Joanna Lumley and other national treasures? Or if that is too crass, we could simply commission a design, something in the tradition of a Ravilious painting or a William Morris tapestry. Anything other than that red, white and blue gate.

Of course my wish won't be granted, so I'll have to make my peace with the Union Jack. Still, the hedgerow makes an intriguing symbol of Britishness, for a variety of reasons. Hedge-fringed gardens and fields are absolutely characteristic of our landscape. As a people, we are known for our reserve, our politeness and our irony. A hedge presents an even, flat surface to the world, while containing dark and thorny depths. Ironic detachment and the famous British 'manners' also tend to be barriers – blank surfaces that may conceal something more heartfelt or dangerous.

Hedges also have an inescapable association with land and property, which lie at the heart of our political and social history. To simplify the national story: in 1066 a gang of Normans of Viking descent came and grabbed owner-ship of the land. Over ensuing centuries, people were thrown off that land in the enclosures and Highland Clearances, both of which transferred land from common use to private ownership.*This process concentrated wealth into the hands of those who came out of it holding large tracts of land.

The enclosures had the positive side-effect of creating many of our modern hedgerows, but they also helped to entrench

---

* Meanwhile the troubles in Ireland can be traced back to land confiscations and plantations of the Tudor and English Civil War periods.

wealth inequality – in many cases the current descendants of those landowners still make money from rents or leases on the land their forebears owned centuries ago. For instance the freeholds for large tracts of land in central London are owned by a handful of families and individuals, including the Duke of Westminster.

It's impossible to escape the importance of land-ownership in our history. Land conveyed political power and status. Only landowners were allowed to vote in parliamentary elections up until the 1832 Reform Act. The result was a legal system that generally favoured landowners over the landless.

So while the hedges that screen our gardens and partition the fields have many practical and ornamental uses, they are also a symbol of historic appropriations and a focal point of separation and conflict between neighbours.

When exploring their history, this aspect of British hedges is often as striking as more everyday concerns. If I propose the hedgerow as a national symbol, I don't mean to suggest that our hedges are always a symbol of unity. On the contrary, there are many ways in which our hedges have historically divided us and kept us apart.

9. The Hedges Between Us
Quarrelsome Neighbours and Private Land

Good fences make good neighbours.
PROVERB, MID-SEVENTEENTH CENTURY

A few years ago, a seventy-two-year-old Lincolnshire man was so annoyed by his neighbour's leylandii hedge, he left the house regularly at night to pee on its roots. The plants started to wither and die as a result. However the hedge's owner set a trap, catching him in the act on camcorder. As a result of this bizarre intervention, the 'Midnight Piddler', as the press dubbed him, spent a day in jail on a charge of criminal damage.

This slightly farcical case epitomises the modern-day morality tale of leylandii, and the disputes this fast-growing plant has caused. Boundary hedges generally belong to one property or the other. If a hedge doesn't belong to you, you don't have the legal right to prune or trim it, and are thus at the mercy of the hedge-owner when it comes to maintenance.

There have been numerous high-profile cases in which hedge disputes spilled over into violence. In Newbury, two sets of warring neighbours exchanged gunfire after a long-running conflict. There were six cases of hedge arson in a single month in Leeds. Llandis Burdon, of Powys, was tragically shot and killed in his own home after a dispute over

The great barrier hedge.

a ten-foot conifer hedge. And in 2003 in Lincoln, the fatal shooting of George Wilson by his neighbour Robert Dickinson was caused by a long-running dispute over the single fifteen-foot-tall leylandii growing in a low hedge. Both men lost their lives as a result, since Dickinson hanged himself in his cell in Lincoln Prison while awaiting trial for murder.

How is it possible for overgrown hedges to inspire such antagonism between neighbours?

Everybody Needs Good Neighbours

Before the birth of agriculture, people lived in tribes, hierarchical social groups that had a sense of territory rather than land-ownership. Woodland clearance and farming helped to make people feel more 'proprietorial' about land. If you had laboured for months or years to clear a field, farmstead or pasture, you would naturally feel entitled to the future fruits of your labour.

When tending your own land, obligations also develop to those using neighbouring land. For instance, in Anglo-Saxon law, farmers were obliged to keep their land enclosed and fences or hedges well maintained. They could be punished for failure to do so, especially if their sheep or cattle escaped. From the earliest farmers onwards, similar codes and conventions concerning shared boundaries were adopted.

In his *Prehistoric Hedges in Cornwall*, Robin Menneer (founder of the Guild of Cornish Hedgers) describes another important aspect of boundaries. Mesolithic families in the area moved between coastal areas in the winter and moorland pastures in the summer, so they needed a way to mark their pasture in their absence:

People are more successful in defending their own recognised territory than in ejecting the owner of another territory; and the more defined is the boundary in physical terms, the easier it is to defend … The greater the effort by a landowner in the fencing or hedging of a boundary, the more committed he is to its defence. The more people there are in a small area, the more threatened is a person's territory and the more important are his hedges. Not only must they be substantial, but they must also appear to be cared for. An air of abandonment shouts to everybody that here is someone who may not be strong enough to defend his boundaries and territory.

As this quote suggests, hedges and other boundary markers don't just mark land-ownership, they also send a message to others about the owner, even in their absence. They have an emotional impact on those who view them, whether from the inside looking out or the outside looking in.

In Robert Frost's poem 'Mending Wall', he describes helping his neighbour repair their adjoining wall, while pondering its purpose. His neighbour has faith in the proverb that equates good fences with good neighbours, but Frost is less sure. He suggests that before he built a wall he would ask who he was walling out or walling in, and whether it might give offence. A gigantic hedge can also send a rather particular message to those excluded or overshadowed by it, one of hostility or indifference. And it is often the tallest hedges that cause problems between neighbours.

Captain Leyland's Monster

Leylandii, also known as the Leyland Cypress, has steadily grown in notoriety through the twentieth century. Planted as a screen, it will grow at an extraordinary speed to create hedges as high as a hundred feet tall. For those who wish to create total privacy this has been an enticing prospect.

However, most people don't want vast hedges overshadowing their gardens. Extraordinarily, *Collins Tree Guide* defines leylandii as 'the most planted and the most hated garden tree' in the UK. Perhaps this is a tad unfair. There are plenty of responsible hedge-owners who would defend it as a useful or beautiful plant in its own right. For instance, in Essex and elsewhere it has been used very effectively to screen gardens from railway lines. But all too often it has been grown without due care and attention, and even for those owners who do wish to keep them under control, the cost of trimming a fully grown leylandii hedge can be an obstacle. Leylandii are greedy drinkers, taking the moisture from surrounding soil, and as a foreign import, they don't even harbour much of our indigenous wildlife. In many respects they are the anti-hedge, a pariah in our 'green and pleasant land'.*

The bastard offspring of two types of cypress native to North-west America, leylandii was first cultivated by C. J. Leyland, a nineteenth-century ship's captain, landowner and amateur botanist. He spotted this unusual hybrid growing wild on his brother-in-law's estate in Scotland, and took some seedlings to his home at Haggerston Castle in Northumberland, a mile or so from the causeway that conveys travellers across the sea to Holy Island.

Leyland was a rather splendid man, who devoted his home life to building a plethora of weird and wonderful buildings at the Castle (now a holiday camp), including an astronomical observatory built into a water tower, and a walled Italian garden. It is a shame that the folly that he is best remembered for is a monstrous tree, rather than the Greek goddesses and pergolas of the walled garden.

The pressure group Hedgeline was set up in response to disputes over leylandii and other hedges, after founder Michael Jones fought a five-year court battle (Stanton vs Jones) over his

---

* Leylandii are also popular in Australia, where they are known as 'Leyton green' or 'spite trees' – Problem Hedges Australia is the campaign group for those affected.

own problem with a neighbour's hedge. He was trying to win the right to trim the giant hedge back to a more reasonable size.

The case was notable for a lengthy digression by the judge investigating the point at which a row of trees can be deemed to be a 'hedge'. This was a crucial point because local law required him to treat the two in different ways. The final judgment was anomalous in that the judge used local bylaws to declare the offending leylandii a 'party hedge'. This gave Michael Jones the right to trim it, but didn't create a precedent for other areas without such bylaws.

Through Hedgeline, he went on to lobby for effective legislation on the problem of hedge disputes. One eventual result was the high hedges section of the 2003 Anti-Social Behaviour Act* which created new provisions for restraining neighbours who allow their hedges to grow too high, with a £1,000 fine to be levied on those who don't comply.

The law is far from perfect. Councils administer it and charge a £600 non-returnable fee if called in for arbitration. This can discourage householders from applying, although the mere threat of arbitration has sometimes been enough to persuade hedge-owners to co-operate. Another catch is the problem of 'staging' – councils can't order a hedge to be killed, so some very high hedges can only be cut down to size in stages over an extended period, in order to keep them alive.

Many members of Hedgeline have suffered years of frustration over the effects of neighbours' hedges, and can tell

---

* This only applies to England and Wales, although there are campaigns in Scotland and Northern Ireland for similar legislation.

stories of blocked light, gardens made arid, blighted property prices, rain shadows, bitter arguments with neighbours and frustrating battles with councils. For instance, Sally Antony wrote to me about her neighbour's high hedges:

> They do take water from the soil ... and it is where I have my vegetable plot, so that's a problem. The main argument I have is that they are much too high for me to safely maintain myself, and I am not able or prepared to pay professionals to do it for me. A few years ago, we borrowed some scaffolding and a chainsaw from a friend and my son did it for me, but he lives away now; and I feel strongly that the neighbours should take responsibility themselves.

She is currently considering whether to risk paying for the council's arbitration procedures.

In Norfolk, Christine Wright had to fight a twenty-four-year battle to have her neighbour's leylandii trees cut down to size. From 1984 to 2008 these overgrown shrubs had blighted her life and prevented her from growing anything more than grass in her garden. As the hedge grew ever taller, her views of the broads disappeared behind a forbidding wall of dark green, and her vegetable garden wilted, robbed of the sunlight it needed. The council finally found in her favour in 2008, so this at least is a case in which the legislation has proved effective.

The distress caused by such hedges arises from our instinctive sense of territory. Whatever the size of our home, we are deeply protective of the space around us. (In the terraced streets of Rochdale where my wife grew up, children playing in the street would often be told to 'go play on your own part', meaning the small segment of pavement that lay directly adjacent to their home.)

Arguments between neighbours often arise because people feel that their territory has been violated. This is why disputes over loud music are so virulent. And high hedges can create a similar sense of intrusion, because they impact directly on us within our own space.

My Patch of Heaven

I have encountered KEEP OUT signs throughout my life as I have wandered the highways and byways of Britain. They always feel like a slap in the face, particularly when they protect unused, fallow land. Large tracts of moorland, Pennine slopes and lowland forest are enclosed and kept private for deer stalking, grouse shooting, or for less immediately apparent reasons. Trespass is a curious concept, which deems it to be an offence to set foot on private land without a lawful reason, even if you don't cause any damage.*

However, the urge for privacy has to be understood from both sides. Trespass is a frustrating law when it keeps us out of areas of natural beauty, but when it comes to our own little patch of land, it seems perfectly reasonable to want to keep strangers at bay. The hedges, fences and walls of town and country are designed to repel intruders and to ensure privacy.

---

* Signs reading 'Trespassers will be prosecuted' were traditionally making a false claim as trespass was a civil offence, not a criminal one, until the Criminal Justice Act created the crime of 'aggravated trespass'.

When we moved to our current home, an ex-council maisonette, the first thing we did was to replace the low, dilapidated fences with taller, six-foot fences. The miniature hedge I planted was an attempt to block off views and access to our back garden at a point where fencing isn't possible.

The children of the street had been accustomed to playing in our garden and we frequently found them roaming through it. One summer day when the door was left open, my wife even found two of them in our kitchen, helping themselves to biscuits. 'Kevin's dad never minded,' they said, in feeble self-defence.

So we spent our first few months here trying to drive home the message that our home and garden were private, not common ground. If it had been possible to conjure up fairy-tale thorn hedges, a padlocked gate and a moat it would have been my preference.

I've never been keen on the idea of communal living. I shudder when I read that modernist architect Le Corbusier proposed housing everyone in identical housing units in blocks of flats in order to improve the human condition. Even worse was his contemporary, Karel Teige, who believed that everyone should be obliged to live communally, sharing dining halls, laundry areas and even bathrooms.

So I don't intend to argue against private ownership and use of land. I want to be able to own the land I live on, and keep other people off it. And I hold the typical British 'bourgeois' view that the ideal home is a private house with a garden, preferably with a hedge tall enough to make it feel secluded and safe.

However, it is interesting to look at how land in Britain first came to be divided into plots that were bought and sold for the exclusive use of the owner, and how the balance between private and common land has changed over time.

The Norman Yoke

Was there ever a historical period when there were no 'neighbours' in the modern sense – when all land was held in common, and there was no difference between 'mine and thine'?

The most basic version of British history suggests a gradual shift of land from common to individual ownership. This is simplistic, but it does contain an element of truth. In particular, the enclosures period saw an ongoing change in land use from communal, open-field systems to a more privatised form of agriculture, in which the new hedges protected fields that were individually owned.

From the thirteenth to the sixteenth centuries it was common for rabble-rousers opposing enclosures to denounce the 'Norman Yoke'. The phrase invokes the idea of an idyllic Saxon period in which everyone had a common stake in the land, which was then usurped by the Normans with their feudal system, under which all land was presumed to belong to the king, or to his barons by grant. Early radicals such as Wat Tyler and the revolting peasants of the fourteenth century or the Levellers, Diggers and Ranters of the Civil War period often expressed the idea of a land without divisions in the rhyme 'when Adam delved and Eve span, who was then the gentleman?' The implication was that the nobility had unfairly attained their wealth off the backs of their fellow countrymen.

This belief in an earlier idyll wasn't confined to English history. Seneca wrote of a time in past history:

> It was impossible for any man to have more or less than another; all things were divided among them without discord ... Not yet had the miser, by hiding his wealth away unused, deprived others of the very necessities of life.

Meanwhile, Virgil described another bygone period:

> *No ploughman tilled the ground,*
> *No fence dividing field from field was found;*
> *When to the common store all gains were brought,*
> *And earth gave freely goods which none had sought.*

There were certainly times when people were able to live off the fat of the land without any great scarcity or competition. In the Mesolithic period in Britain, giant herds of animals provided a seemingly inexhaustible food source. It was only when the herds declined, and mankind started to farm, that people needed to mark out permanent territory at all.

However, this didn't automatically lead to private ownership of land. By the Iron Age, land was under tribal control, and there was a rudimentary monetary system, but land wasn't bought and sold by individuals – instead it was controlled by tribes or extended family groups.

The Romans brought a complex system of individual land ownership to Britain. Under Roman law, jointly owned land could be divided into distinct ownership units. This made it easier for the spivs and chancers of the Roman Empire to make money from buying and selling land – after the British invasion Roman generals were granted large areas of the country and they often sold plots of land on to profit-seeking speculators.

It is unclear whether individual land-ownership persisted in the post-Roman period – in the chaotic aftermath, land was probably just occupied by those who were able to defend and retain it. The medieval protesters who invoked the 'Norman Yoke' were thus assuming that between the Roman and Norman invasions, land returned to the utopia of common ownership.

On closer examination, this turns out to be something of a romanticisation. The Anglo-Saxon period was far from idyllic for the ordinary people of Britain, and only a fraction of the land was held in common.

There were originally three distinctions of land in Saxon law. 'Folk land' belonged to the nation and was under the control of the king and the Witan (the ruling council); 'family land' was the land around the house and garden which belonged to an individual kinship group; 'common land' was used collectively, and included the streets and squares of a village and shared grazing land.

Folk land could be held and used by individuals or families, in return for taxes, but, crucially, it could not be bought or sold. And family land couldn't be transferred out of the kinship group, so there was no means by which any individual could build up a significant holding of land. Open-field farming was becoming widespread in this period, but there were no large-scale estates.

'Folkright' was the idea that the law represented the will of the tribe, or the people. Under folkright, land was treated as a common asset, to be used by a tribe or family. The only way this could be changed was by 'privilege' – laws or concessions referring to particular individuals and giving them rights that outweighed folkright.*

In the seventh century a new concept – 'book land' – entered the picture. This was land granted by a charter that could be transferred between individuals. The motivation for this was the arrival of Christianity. Churches and monasteries wanted to control their own land and had inherited Roman legal traditions that suggested that the monarchy and Church were entitled to privileges derived from God that trumped the will of the people.

The Church started to petition the monarch to grant it land. Book land was granted through a charter in return for commitments to maintain local roads or other obligations. These are the charters that are still used by landscape historians to identify which hedges, fields and roads existed at this time.

Book land made it easier for an individual to become wealthy. The more devious Saxons started to seek charters under the pretence of building religious institutions. By AD 731 we find Bede complaining to the Archbishop of York about 'pretended monks', scammers who were enriching themselves by getting land from charters but failing to actually build the promised priories and monasteries. The shift towards book land allowed individuals to build up larger estates. At the start of the eleventh century, one Wulfric Spott, who founded a monastery at Burton-on-Trent, had seventy-two estates,

---

* 'Privilege' and 'private' come from the same root words meaning 'individual, one's own'.

making him a seriously wealthy man. He owned much of what is now South Yorkshire – in his will he bequeathed the manors of Barlborough, Beighton, Clowne, Duckmanton, Eckington, Mosborough and Whitwell to a local member of the nobility.

So when the Normans took over from the Anglo-Saxons, we already had a system that was somewhat 'feudal'. However, the Normans did formalise this by treating all land as being in the gift of the monarch. From the conquest onwards, private ownership of land, stemming from royal grant, became ever more entrenched. Under Norman law, primogeniture meant that the eldest son inherited the estate, allowing individuals to become owners of increasing amounts of land. (The invention of locks and keys in the twelfth century was another step towards a greater expectation of privacy in ordinary homes.)

Subsequent shifts in power between king, barons and freemen created a dominant landowning class, which survived the gradual collapse of the feudal system into a more mercantilist and imperial economy and became the 'landed gentry'.

Beyond the Hedge

Whether we rent or own our homes, we are legally entitled to the 'quiet enjoyment' of our property. We expect the neighbours to respect our privacy, and to stay on their side of the garden hedge.

The buying and selling of parcels of land from the Saxon period onwards did not create the problem of neighbour disputes, but it did help to shape a society in which neighbours could be strangers. In the distant past, families were separated from their neighbours by hedges and walls, just as they are today. However, before the development of larger towns and cities, neighbours were either kin or had been neighbours for a long time.

This is one obvious way that the relationship between neighbours changed over the centuries. Settlements increased in size, from villages to towns and cities, people became more mobile, and property changed hands more often. Today it is not uncommon to live next to complete strangers, even in villages. In our cities many people don't even know the names of their closest neighbours.

The word 'alienation' originally referred to the ability to transfer legal ownership of a thing to someone else, from the Latin *alienus*, meaning 'of or belonging to another person or place'. 'Alienation' of privately owned land, which became gradually more common through British history, is thus part of the same process that leads to 'alienation' in society, the idea that we do not feel part of the community around us.

The relationship between individual and community is a very emotive issue – it is one of the dividing lines in British politics with the 'right wing' tending to emphasise individual rights and responsibilities and the 'left wing' tending to emphasise those of the community.

But the way that neighbours relate to each other has a more immediate significance. Writing about the problems of hedge disputes recently, Will Cohu wrote:

The leylandii is more than a means to secure our privacy. It allows us to enjoy the fantasy that next door does not exist. But if we cannot see our neighbours, they cannot see us either, and we can then become monstrous in their minds.

I think this hits the nail squarely on the head. In modern Britain, many of us are isolated, or alienated, from our neighbours. When we use the garden hedge as a barrier to communication, as something to hide behind, we become more estranged from the community and we lose the desire or ability to solve problems collectively.

Our neighbours were once insiders, part of the same group or tribe, but now they are often seen as outsiders,* aliens, others. As a result the garden hedge is no longer something over which we talk to neighbours – instead it is the barrier that separates us from them.

At the same time as being outsiders, our neighbours are physically very close to us. Naomi King Li, a psychologist who specialises in mediation, says that 'people get incredibly upset in neighbourhood disputes because you are right next door to someone. You cannot get away or just switch off because it is there 24 hours a day.'

It is notable how often in hedge disputes the warring neighbours weren't on speaking terms in the first place. The 'Midnight Piddler', for instance, hadn't directly spoken to his neighbour for eight years. In many cases one or both of the combatants was clearly behaving unreasonably or obnoxiously, but you wonder if they would have behaved the same way towards someone they were able to communicate with more easily.

Jesus once advised us to love our neighbours as ourselves – in fact he extended the Old Testament admonition to love

---

* The words 'insider' and 'outsider' are fascinating in themselves – to be an outsider is to be excluded from the security of an enclosed community, to be outside the boundaries and barriers that protect insiders.

your neighbour, which might be taken to refer only to your kin or tribe, to the stronger idea that everyone (even those pesky Samaritans) should be treated as neighbours.

While Britain has been a Christian country since the dark ages, we have generally tended more towards a watered down version of Jesus's teaching, as captured in George Herbert's rendition of an old proverb: 'Love your neighbour, yet pull not down your hedge.'

10. This Land is My Land
Private Property

There is something that Governments care for far more than human life, and that is the security of property, and so it is through property that we shall strike the enemy.
EMMELINE PANKHURST

I magine this. I plant a hedge around a patch of vacant land. I dig and clear that land, I conquer the weeds and cultivate edible plants, and I build myself a shack there.

Do I now own that patch of land? If so, do I have the right to stop other people using it? These are the philosophical questions at the heart of land-ownership.

In British history, the ability to acquire and retain private land became gradually accepted as a fundamental right. As the Empire grew, locals such as the Native Americans – who had no concept of land-ownership – were bewildered when the British turned up, planted a flag and claimed a patch of land as theirs by right. (Luckily we were well armed, and backed up by gunboats, so we tended to win this particular debate as we roamed around the world.)

John Locke's identification of the basic rights of 'Life, Liberty and Property' was widely adopted as a fundamental political truth, and helped to shape the political landscape of the last few centuries. The freedom to trade, to acquire capital and lay claim to resources was fundamental to the growth of Britain as an industrial and military power.

However, Locke's approach is not just a simplistic justification of property rights. In his *Second Treatise on Government*, he starts from exactly the same observation as Gerrard Winstanley and the Diggers (see pages 101–3), by accepting that God gave the earth to all men in common. On this basis, he suggests that the only thing that gives me any right to ownership of the patch of land I have cultivated is the labour I have put into shaping it.

He then argues that it would only be fair for anyone to own the amount of land they need for their own use, which would rule out any kind of hoarding of land, or the ownership of surplus land on which you charge rent.

However, Locke restricts this interpretation to the early period of mankind, before the use of money. When goods were bartered, there was not much point in hoarding resources, since most of the immediate necessities of life, in terms of food, water and shelter are perishable. It was only when monetary systems came into use, whether they were based on gold, silver, seashells, tally sticks or whatever, that hoarding became more worthwhile. Money made the unlimited acquisition of wealth possible.

So Locke has argued himself into a corner. He doesn't want to say that you shouldn't hoard more property and money than you have a reasonable need for. Apart from anything else, this would amount to a denunciation of not just the aristocracy (whose money often derived from rents) but also the monarchy. Locke was a smart guy but he was no revolutionary.

Instead, he rather fudges the argument, by claiming that the fundamental purpose of society is to protect private property:

> The reason why men enter into society, is the preservation of their property; and the end why they choose and authorize a legislative, is, that there may be laws made, and rules set, as guards and fences to the properties of all the members of the society.

In other words we only have laws and society in the first place so that we can protect our land and other possessions with 'guards and fences'.

This rather circular argument allows Locke to discard the implications of the first part of his argument and to assert that property is a natural right within society. (To be fair, he does acknowledge that unlimited property accumulation isn't compatible with a fair distribution of wealth – he suggests governments might need to regulate this somehow, in order to limit inequality, but he doesn't suggest a way of doing this.)

The problem in Locke's approach is that land is a limited natural resource. Going back to my hedged plot of land, what created its value? It was a combination of my labour and the 'God-given' land, which Locke already accepted was given to all men in common. So there is a private and common element in its value. And by using this land, I am preventing others from using it – all the more so if I stop them from setting foot on it.

Simply to say that I own this land because I have tended it doesn't take the common, public dimension into account. But on the other hand, the labour I have put into the land surely does give me a right to expect to be able to keep the fruits of that labour for myself.

So how should the public and private aspects of land be reconciled? I want to briefly look at three alternative approaches to this problem that have been suggested in the past: communal ownership, distributism and Georgism.

The Communal Approach

When the Diggers set up camp on St George's Hill, they were rejecting the idea that any individual had the right to own land. Their leader Gerrard Winstanley said:

> The poorest man hath as true a title and just a right to land as the richest man … by the Law of Creation it is everyone's and not a single one's.

The idea that land belonged exclusively to no one was a common belief in tribal societies, for instance the pre-colonial inhabitants of Australasia or Africa. Communal ownership of land was also Plato's preferred option in the *Republic*. A later version was the communist theory that all land belonged to the state.

Apart from the historical problems of Marxism, I think that communal ownership is a flawed solution. It ignores the fact that those who currently hold land feel a reasonable entitlement to that land based on their labour and the labour of their ancestors.

The anarchist thinker Proudhon once claimed that 'property is theft'. Simply rejecting all private property in this way seems too simplistic to me. I don't think property can be either a 'natural right' or 'theft'. The idea of property rights seems to be based on a perfectly understandable attachment to the things you have made or helped to shape, so instead we need to look for some kind of compromise between the private and public interests.

Fair Shares

Some thinkers have focused on a different part of Locke's argument – the fudge he uses to justify people acquiring unlimited wealth in a monetary system. If it is self-evident to him that it would be unfair to hoard land in a barter economy, why shouldn't the same apply to a monetary economy? If a communal system wouldn't work, shouldn't land at least be divided more equally, so that everyone has a 'fair share'?

One sixteenth-century Cornish statute that was aimed at negating the ill-effects of enclosures stated that there should be one cottage for every four acres of land and that one family should occupy that cottage. (This initiative was largely ignored by landowners, who simply found ways to circumvent the rules.) Later, from the 1880s onwards, the slogan 'three acres and a cow' was used as a battlecry for those who felt that everyone should be allowed access to sufficient land for self-sufficiency. (Even today there is enough land in the UK for approximately an acre per person, if the land were to be evenly divided.)

But how do we find a feasible way to give people a more equal stake? Alternative approaches to this dilemma have been proposed by movements such as guild socialism, the co-operative movement and syndicalism.

One interesting approach was 'distributism', advocated by thinkers such as G. K. Chesterton and Dorothy Day. The distributists accepted private property as a good thing that gave people a harmonious relationship with their environment. But they argued that everything should be done at more modest scales – in small companies rather than massive corporations, and in family farms rather than larger conglomerates. They saw it as unfair for anyone to hold an excessive amount of property. For instance, Chesterton argued:

> One would think, to hear people talk, that the Rothschilds and the Rockefellers were on the side of property. But obviously they are the enemies of property because they are enemies of their own limitations. They do not want their own land; but other people's ... It is the negation of property that the Duke of Sutherland should have all the farms in one estate; just as it would be the negation of marriage if he had all our wives in one harem.

In many European countries, revolutions in the eighteenth and nineteenth centuries led to land being distributed over a wide range of small-scale proprietors. For instance, the French Revolution seized land from the aristocracy, then the Napoleonic Code changed the law to spread land inheritance more evenly. However Britain never had a revolution of this sort. The Civil War was, if anything, a victory for existing landowners, as it accelerated the rate of enclosures. As a result, across Europe, land tends to be more evenly divided than in the UK.

But, short of a full-blown revolution, how do you ration or redistribute land without infringing on current property rights? Do you impose limits on ownership? Expect people to generously reduce their wealth to benefit others?

It is hard to see how this worthy aim could be achieved in practice.

The Landlord's Game

The thinker who perhaps came closest to squaring the circle of land-ownership is the nineteenth-century American economist Henry George. He observed that wealth tends to flow to landowners through rents, and that the increasing wealth that capitalism brings also brings extremes of poverty.

He argued that, since land is a natural resource, everyone has equal claims to its bounty. However, rather than suggest a simplistic communal approach he recognised that part of the value of land is dependent on the activities of the owner. So he tried to find a way to acknowledge that everyone owns what they create, while everything found in nature belongs equally to everyone.

His solution was to suggest the single land tax: income tax would be abolished and all tax would be raised from landowners instead. Rather than taking privately owned land into communal ownership, the rights of owners to use land fruitfully would be recognised. The tax would be based on the unimproved value of the land, meaning that you would be entitled to hold on to any increase in value created by improving, cultivating or building on the land.

At the same time, hoarding of land would be discouraged, and enterprise (in the form of labour and effort) would be better rewarded. This would also have the virtue of making speculation in land less attractive. Excessive property speculation is one of the major causes of credit bubbles, of which the 2007–8 financial crisis was just the latest example.

Henry George was influential in his time, but he is best known now for a slightly odd consequence of his work. One of his followers, Lizzie Magie, invented a board game called the Landlord's Game, to show how society was a rigged game, geared to favour the landowners. This turned into the modern game Monopoly, which teaches children the same moral, albeit in a less evangelistic manner.

It's hard to know how well Georgism would work in practice as it has never been fully implemented. However, the British government did come remarkably close to enacting his ideas. In 1909, Lloyd George wanted to adopt the land value tax. He was a strong critic of the concentration of property and wealth, at one point asking 'by what right are ten thousand people owners of the soil in this country and the rest of us trespassers in the land of our birth?'

Landowners in the House of Lords were fiercely opposed to it and dug their heels in. They were so determined to prevent its passage that they gambled on the status and very existence of the upper house by persistently rejecting the so-called 'People's Budget'. The impasse was only resolved in 1911 when the Lords accepted restrictions on their ability to veto future legislation in return for the land tax being dropped.

So we can't know what difference Lloyd George's land tax would have made. The only thing we do know is how determined our nation's lords and landowners were to defeat it.

This Green and Pleasant Land

It's interesting to ponder what might have been, but in the end we have the system we have. Private land that can be bought and sold is treated as a natural right. Income is taxed more heavily than property. And most British people would defend the status quo in spite of the fact that very few of us really own our homes, given that a large proportion of them are either owned by lenders (via mortgages) or by freeholders, since a leasehold is only a kind of long-term tenancy.

This system of land-ownership shaped the British landscape, for better or for worse. Even towns and suburbs tend to follow the patterns of the old fields – in many cases, it was individual farms and fields on the edge of towns that were gradually sold to property developers. This piecemeal development led to modern streets that follow ancient hedge lines and green lanes. These patterns reveal the ebb and flow of land-ownership across the centuries. Primogeniture, enclosure and alienation of land gave us the great country houses with parks that we enjoy today. The beauty of our countryside is arguably a direct result of how few people owned it, as we ended up with wide expanses of rural land rather than scattered plots in smallholdings.

However, the flipside of this is that the towns and villages became relatively cramped. In some cases this was an extreme process. For instance Nottingham in the nineteenth century was a growing city where the surrounding land could not be bought for development (ironically because it was still in common ownership). Seriously crowded slums developed in the city as a result.

We have been subject to restrictions on land use and excluded from the great estates over the centuries, so we have ended up with relatively concentrated areas of population. In the twentieth century this process was exacerbated by planning restrictions, green belt protection and a gradual reduction in building standards* including the number of housing units allowed per acre and smaller room sizes.

This isn't an especially overpopulated island. Over 90 per cent of the land is habitable, flat, temperate and has accessible water. However in particular places it can feel extremely crowded, and this is because a high proportion of the population live in a small proportion of the land.

Maybe it is precisely because we are crammed into relatively small spaces that we are so protective of the space we do control. We don't have the generous plots of land that often go with suburban and even urban homes in American and Australian cities. Instead we mostly live in houses, apartments and flats with modest amounts of space dividing us. Most people have gardens in which it is possible to see and hear the neighbours.

And so we huddle behind our hedges, trying to pretend that those pesky neighbours aren't there.

The Other Side of the Hedge

So what would it take to get us to come out from behind our hedges? It's hard to give a general answer to this question, but I can give a personal one.

---

* We are currently the only European country with no minimum size regulations for new-build property, one reason why many newly built houses and apartments are almost unusable and lack storage space.

Soon after I had enclosed the garden in my home, my old gate started to fall off its hinges. I set out to mend it one day, with my rickety box of tools, and my neighbour came out to help. When my drill turned out to be inadequate, he fetched his from inside, and after an hour or so we had done a far better job than I could have managed alone. He could easily have taken offence at my rather curmudgeonly arrival in the neighbourhood, but instead chose to help me out.

Moments like this focus your mind on the value of community. Like many people, I treasure my privacy, and have sometimes been too quick to block the neighbours out. However, I have gradually got to know people on my street, through feeding each other's cats, campaigning against local school closures, shovelling snow in an icy spell and so on. Once my daughter started school, school-gates acquaintances added to the circle of people I knew. She made friends of her own age on the street so we ended up with a houseful of children once again, although this time with our consent.

It's when you share experiences with the neighbours, or discuss local problems and issues, that you stop treating them as strangers. This is one reason why the ongoing loss of local pubs seems a sad thing to me – for generations, neighbours who might otherwise only ever nod at each other in the street got to meet up in the local. A sense of community can't be imposed, but it helps if there are locations where people can meet, whether they be pubs, community centres, churches or local shops.

In spite of the zeal for social engineering in post-war Britain, the planners of new housing often made a very specific mistake. They designed units of housing to contain families in 'little boxes' but they neglected communal areas. Many estates contained no pubs or community centres and, at best, a token arcade of shops. The open green spaces were bleak and unfriendly. People who were relocated to the new post-war housing after slum clearance often missed the friendly street activity of their old homes, and felt isolated in the new houses, in spite of the improved living conditions.

Of course, some people have neighbours so dreadful, or local surroundings so unwelcoming, that it can seem impossible to let your guard down. It's easy to make worthy suggestions about community involvement, but life isn't always that simple.

However, even the toughest estates and areas of the country do tend to take a turn for the better when there is some kind of local activity or organisation. Kids in hoodies on street corners can look slightly less intimidating if you are on speaking terms with their families.

We don't always need to choose between privacy and community – perhaps instead we can look for the right balance between the two. There is no overnight cure for the alienation many of us feel from our communities, whether we live behind the front doors of an isolated housing estate, in a leafy village or behind the privet hedges of suburbia. But if we want to keep a sense of community alive, we do occasionally need to find ways to come out from behind our hedges and get to know the people they conceal.

The Customs Hedge of India

See-Saw-Jack in the hedge
Which is the way to London Bridge?
MOTHER GOOSE

British émigrés have often taken the culture of hedge-making around the world with them. The Eastern Cape of South Africa, where the 1820 English settlers landed, contains areas of patchwork landscape notably reminiscent of England and unknown elsewhere in South Africa. In the same period, William Cobbett, in one of his sojourns in America, expended considerable energy attempting to persuade the locals of the virtues of hedges. In *The American Gardener*, he waxed lyrical about hawthorn in particular:

> This Haw-Thorn is the favourite plant of England: it is seen as a flowering shrub in all gentlemen's pleasure-grounds; it is the constant ornament of paddocks and parks; the first appearance of its blossoms is hailed by old and young as the sign of pleasant weather; its branches of flowers are emphatically called 'May', because, according to the Old Style, its time of blooming was about the first of May, which, in England is called 'May-Day'; in short, take away the Haw-Thorn, and you take away the greatest beauty of the English fields and gardens, and not a small one from

English rural poetry. And why should America not possess this most beautiful and useful plant?

At the height of the British Empire, the civil servants and soldiers of the Raj built what may well be the world's longest ever hedge. It was planted as a barrier to enforce the salt tax. Many countries, including China and France, have taxed salt over the centuries, and the British weren't the first to do so in India. However, salt is a nutritional necessity, all the more so in India where many of the population are vegetarian and receive little or no salt in their daily diet, so the salt tax was regarded by many as iniquitous.

We have Roy Moxham, a conservator at the University of London Library, to thank for saving the bizarre story of the Customs Hedge for posterity. In 1995, he came across a reference to it in an antiquarian book. As a result he became increasingly obsessed with verifying its existence and locating it. He scoured nineteenth-century maps for clues, made a series of journeys to India, and finally wrote *The Great Hedge of India* about his quest.

What Roy had stumbled across was not just a quaint story about hedges, but a remarkable insight into the British occupation of India. The tax collectors' activities were being stymied by widespread salt smuggling. In 1840 they started to build a fortified line, strengthened with manned stations to try and combat this. The full guarded customs line would eventually be 2,504 miles long.

The line was initially made of walls and fences, but an increasing portion came to be made up of hedges. At first these were dead hedges of thorn bushes and brushwood.

However it was found that the bushes rerooted and the live hedges that resulted were hardier and more impenetrable. As a result the British spent decades planting up and maintaining the hedge along the customs line. After experimenting with various species, it was largely made up of dwarf Indian plum, with prickly pear in drier areas, all intermingled with other species including acacia and thorny creepers. About 1,500 miles of the full line was made up of dry or green hedge. The live portion ended up about 800 miles long.

The salt tax caused a great deal of suffering – there were severe famines while the tax was in force, and iodine deficiency exacerbated many avoidable diseases. But still, you can't help but be amazed by the ingenuity and efficiency with which the Customs Hedge was created. In its most complete form, it was a formidable barrier between ten and fifteen feet tall. It continued for mile after mile across the countryside from modern-day Pakistan down past Delhi and Agra in the heart of India. And while some sections remained incomplete it was extremely effective for hundreds of miles of its length, and allowed the boundary to be patrolled by far fewer soldiers than would otherwise have been required.

The hedge was abandoned in 1879 when the British achieved a monopoly on salt production in the subcontinent. This made the Customs Line redundant and it mostly disappeared over the following century. Roy's journeys to India initially found no trace of the hedge and he came close to abandoning his quixotic task.

Eventually he found one clear remnant of the line between Chakanagar and Pali Ghar in Etawah District. A raised bank marked the path of the *Parmat Lain* and on one section he was delighted to finally identify grown-out remains of the hedge itself – thorny acacias and Indian plum trees, no longer making a solid barrier, having reseeded and spread over the years, but clearly in the correct position to be the final remnants of the original hedge.

11. Keeping up with the Joneses
Hedges and Snobbery in the British Garden

In my bedroom in Italy, I dreamed of English gardens.
A million shades of rain-fed green. Pink peonies as big
as rugby balls. A duck pond and a hedge carved in the
shape of a peacock.

THE SECRET SHOPPER'S REVENGE, KATE HARRISON

We all notice different things in a garden. For some it is the flowers, for others the lawns, the planting patterns, the trees or the ornamentation. The first thing I look for is the hedges. They play a crucial role because they provide the structure, the permanent shape against which other, more transient elements are juxtaposed. You can visit a garden in the depths of winter, long after the flowers have wilted and died, and still admire the architectural qualities of the hedging.

In garden history, hedges are often relegated to a footnote, granted only condescending references that treat them as a minor element of background scenery. But classic horticultural fashions were often rooted in the innovative use of hedging, which created the underlying forms and structures in the garden.

So I feel it is my duty here to push hedges back into the limelight, and to stress their fundamental importance in the story of British gardens.

221

The Dawn of the Garden Snob

In the Tudor period gardening was becoming steadily more popular. After a couple of centuries in which Britain's main pastimes were war, famine and plague, life started to improve slightly in the late fifteenth century. Britain's power as a trading and military nation became slowly greater, and the gardens of the great estates were the first to reflect the increasing peace and prosperity.

Renaissance ideas were spreading across Europe, with the cultures of Ancient Greece and Rome being viewed as models for a new golden age. The Roman garden, with its detailed use of hedging and topiary, was a particular inspiration.

The formal garden of this period was intended to be viewed from aloft, rather than walked through. Many were designed to be seen from the upper floor of the castle or stately home they were attached to, and there was also a fashion for mounts, artificial hills, from the peak of which the perspectives and patterns of the garden could be viewed to best effect. Hedges played a fundamental role, creating the overall pattern in the formal gardens that were thus viewed. Topiary and intricately patterned borders provided further layers of detail in the design.

The term 'knot' was first recorded in reference to a British garden in 1494. In a knot garden, low hedges (usually box) created elaborate designs, resembling the complicated patterns that can be made by knotting cord or rope. The spaces were filled with anything from flowers to vegetables, coloured earth, gravel and turf. The combination of hedging and infill was used to create a bold pattern to please the eye.

In an era when nurseries selling bedding plants had not developed, and there were fewer species available to gardeners than today, it was necessary to resort to coloured objects other than plants to create these patterns.

The first Tudor monarch, Henry VII, was not especially grandiose in his tastes but he did import the ornate horticultural styles of Burgundy to his palace at Richmond. There he had a fine garden:

> With royal knots allayed and herbed; many marvellous beasts, such as lions, dragons and such other of divers kind, properly fashioned and carved in the ground … with many vines, seeds and strange fruit, right goodly beset.

Through the reigns of the fatter Henry who followed and Queen Elizabeth, the trend for formal gardening became gradually more extravagant. Henry VIII had elaborate gardens laid out at Hampton Court, the palace which he had purloined from Cardinal Wolsey when Wolsey fell from favour. They may have featured a hedge maze, planted for either Wolsey or Henry VIII – the current maze was planted from 1685 onwards, but it is thought to have been on the site of an earlier one.

Late in Elizabeth's reign, in 1599, the topiary in these gardens was described by a German visitor as 'all manner of shapes, men and women, half men and half horse, sirens, serving maids with baskets, French lilies and delicate crenellations all round.' (The 'battlement' hedge was clearly in fashion even in the Elizabethan period.)

In the sixteenth and early seventeenth century, the gardens of stately houses were elaborate affairs with decorative areas divided by hedges. Mazes and labyrinths made of turf or hedges became increasingly popular. The 'parterre' was also imported from France in the seventeenth century. This is a more complex feature than a knot. Low hedges are used to separate and delineate beds in a level garden area. The individual beds might be knots, or solid masses of a single element, but the distinctive feature is that the beds form a wider overall pattern when viewed together. Parterres on an epic scale can be seen today at Hampton Court in Surrey and Drummond Castle Gardens in Perthshire, amongst other places across the country.

Such grand gardens required a fantastic amount of upkeep, as they relied on precise angles and perspectives in the hedges and borders as well as in the elaborate topiaries. But there was also a steady growth in enthusiasm for gardening at a more modest level. Over the centuries, the basic arts of gardening had developed in monastery gardens, rural cottages and

Design for Lord Burleigh's Maze at Theobalds
(which was destroyed in the Civil War).

urban plots as well as the great houses and castles. While the wealthier classes had used gardens as status symbols and entertainments, ordinary people had mostly just seen them as a source of food.

However, from the Tudor period onwards the idea that your garden reflected your personality and status became much more widespread.* As kings and queens copied the styles of their continental neighbours, the aristocracy started to ape royal fashion. And the new styles also filtered down to the common people, at least to those who had the necessary space and time.

Gardening as a hobby became a firmly rooted part of the general culture of Britain. Shakespeare was counting on the horticultural knowledge of his audience when he compared the nation to a disorderly garden with neglected hedges and knots in *Richard II*:

> *When our sea-walled garden, the whole land,*
> *Is full of weeds, her fairest flowers chok'd up,*
> *Her fruit-trees all unprun'd, her hedges ruin'd*
> *Her knots disorder'd and her wholesome herbs*
> *Swarming with caterpillars ...*

The idea that your garden made a statement about who you were gave the snobbish tendency of British society a new outlet. The same drive that sent some abroad to acquire spices, slaves, precious metals and diamonds inspired plant

---

* Jenny Uglow makes this point in *A Little History of British Gardening.*

collectors to roam across the world, bringing home more and more exotic species. As trade and colonisation created the foundations of the British Empire, new seeds, new plants, new trees started to make their presence felt at home, and to become the latest garden status symbols.

And as the latest species and styles appeared, those of a snobbish inclination naturally became competitive about their gardens, just as neighbours today peer over garden hedges and mock the pretensions and shortcomings of one another's little plots.*

The Bonfire of the Topiaries

A natural result of competition amongst gardeners was the ebb and flow of horticultural fashions. By the early seventeenth century, the knots and topiaries of the wealthy gardens were being copied by the 'lower classes'. Individual topiaries, knots created on a small scale and even modest parterres became common sights in the gardens of ordinary homes.

And no sooner did they appear than someone somewhere started to sneer at them for being pretentious or passé.

In 1625 Francis Bacon wrote condescendingly about current fashions in his essay 'Of Gardens'. Of knots he says: 'they be but toys, you may see as good sights many times in tarts'. Topiary is similarly dismissed – 'I for my part do not like images cut in juniper or other garden stuff; they be for children.'

---

* It was recently reported that many potential homebuyers are put off if a property has privet or leylandii hedges, as both are considered 'common' or 'downmarket'.

Even without these childish pleasures, Bacon's ideal garden sounds ornate enough:

> The garden is best to be square, encompassed on all the four sides with a stately arched hedge. The arches to be upon pillars of carpenter's work, of some ten foot high, and six foot broad; and the spaces between of the same dimension with the breadth of the arch. Over the arches let there be an entire hedge of some four foot high, framed also upon carpenter's work; and upon the upper hedge, over every arch, a little turret, with a belly, enough to receive a cage of birds: and over every space between the arches some other little figure, with broad plates of round colored glass gilt, for the sun to play upon. But this hedge I intend to be raised upon a bank, not steep, but gently sloped, of some six foot, set all with flowers.

Ghastly as this sounds, it is an indication that people were starting to use gardens in a different way, as it is evidently designed to be walked through, rather than surveyed from a static viewpoint. As people started to promenade through gardens more, hedges took on new roles. Viewed from ground level, a path between hedges or an archway through the greenery created elements of surprise and secrecy. The hedge was now the portal through which you discovered new elements of a garden, as well as the backdrop to the plants and flowers. Gardens also became more expansive now that they no longer needed to be designed to be viewed from a single point.

Bacon's pretentious disdain was not enough to demolish the fashion for knots and topiary, although more naturalistic and romantic styles developed through the seventeenth century, with hedges used to define and separate areas and to create avenues.

Topiary suffered a more telling blow in the next century from Alexander Pope's scathing satire, 'Verdant Sculpture'. Purporting to be selling the creations of a town gardener who represents the 'advancement of a politer sort of ornament in the Villas and Gardens adjacent to this great city' Pope suggests that

> the world stands much in need of a virtuoso Gardiner, who has a turn to Sculpture, and is thereby capable of improving upon the ancients of his profession, in the imagery of Ever-greens. My correspondant is arrived to such perfection that he also cutteth family pieces of men, women, or children. Any ladies that please may have their own effigies in Myrtle, or their husband's in Horn-beam.

Pope proceeds to the 'catalogue of greens', which would ring painfully true for anyone who had seen the suburban topiary he was skewering:

- Adam and Eve in Yew; Adam a little shattered by the fall of the Tree of Knowledge in the Great Storm; Eve and the Serpent very flourishing.
- Noah's ark in Holly, the ribs a little damaged for want of water.
- The Tower of Babel, not yet finished.
- St. George in Box; his arm scarce long enough, but will be in a condition to stick the Dragon by next April.

- A green Dragon of the same, with a tail of Ground-Ivy for the present.

N. B. These two not to be sold separately.

- Edward the Black Prince in Cypress.
- A Laurestine Bear in Blossom, with a Juniper Hunter in Berries.
- A pair of Giants, stunted, to be sold cheap.
- A Queen Elizabeth in Phyllirea, a little inclining to the green sickness, but of full growth.
- Another Queen Elizabeth in Myrtle, which was very forward, but miscarried by being too near a Savine.
- An old Maid of honour in Wormwood.
- A topping Ben Johnson in Laurel.
- Divers eminent modern Poets in Bays, somewhat blighted, to be disposed of a pennyworth.
- A quick-set Hog shot up into a Porcupine, by being forgot a week in rainy weather.
- A Lavender Pigg, with Sage growing in his belly.
- A pair of Maidenheads in Fir, in great forwardness.

It was not just topiary that drew Pope's ire. He was an enemy of traditional styles and formal gardening in general. In a 1713 article he argued for gardens with the 'amiable simplicity of unadorned nature'. His call for naturalism would help to inspire the landscape gardening movement that would lead to the destruction of so many classic hedged gardens.

Pope himself was something of a fashion victim. At his Twickenham villa he created a famous grotto, studded with alabaster, marbles, ores and crystals, several mirrors and a camera obscura. He reportedly said that: 'Were it to have nymphs as well – it would be complete in everything.' Clearly the age of minimalism was still a long way off.

The grotto led to his garden, which was designed in a pastoral style, based on his ideas of picturesque art. It was supposed to invoke the unspoilt countryside, something through which you could ramble while experiencing a sequence of theatrical scenes.

Under the influence of such ideas, fashion turned away from the European style of parterres, hedged avenues and fountains, towards romantic whimsy and the picturesque. It had started to become fashionable to admire the landscape. Or at least, an idealised version of the landscape. While later country-lovers such as William Wordsworth genuinely appreciated the rugged countryside, the early eighteenth-century Grand Tourists tended to appreciate the pastoral landscape paintings of artists such as Poussin, Salvatore Rosa and Claude Lorrain and wanted to recreate such imagery back home in Britain.

This aesthetic approach motivated the landscape gardening revolution of Capability Brown and his imitators. Over the course of a generation or two in the mid-eighteenth century, a large proportion of British stately homes had their parterres and fountains demolished, their knots dug up and their beautiful (and not so beautiful) topiaries chopped down and burned on the bonfire of history. Brown had an unreasonable dislike of hedge mazes and they rarely survived his improvements.

The new fashion was so widespread that it is now unusual to find a formal garden such as Levens Hall that survived the cull. Brown alone was responsible for complete redesigns of Stowe, Blenheim Palace, Warwick Castle, Harewood House, Bowood House and Milton Abbey, amongst many others.

His modus operandi was to completely re-imagine the gardens of the aristocracy, for a suitably hefty fee. His workers created new landscapes, levelling the mounts of formal gardens, and building new, 'naturally' contoured hills by shifting tons of earth from place to place. Hedges and fences were torn down in favour of ha-has, concealed barriers that left no obstacle to views of the countryside beyond.

Trees were uprooted and replanted to fit the landscape gardeners' visions of rural beauty. Water features were of great importance and many new curving ponds and serpentine lakes were dug and irrigated. As well as these pseudo-natural features, faked ruins, follies and grottoes, and classical 'temples', statues and obelisks were added, in order to complete the arcadian vision.

Of course this was not real landscape, just a slightly odd simulation, and didn't imply that the creators of these gardens genuinely loved the British countryside, or its residents. Pretend hermits and statues of nymphs were all very well, but *hoi polloi* were not part of the plan. At Stowe, the impressive garden was created by destroying the village and relocating the residents a mile away – apparently they were only allowed back in if they wore smocks to make them more picturesque.*

Hedges, especially decorative ones, were mostly excluded from the landscape garden as they were regarded as functional and man-made. The garden designer Humphry Repton

---

* This anecdote is related by Rebecca Solnit in *Wanderlust*. It was not an isolated case – for instance, during John Vanbrugh's creation of the gardens at Castle Howard an entire medieval village was demolished.

disliked hedges, lines of trees and windbreaks as much as Brown, describing them as 'a curtain drawn across the most interesting schemes'. The real countryside beyond the garden might be criss-crossed with the new enclosure hedges that were carving up the landscape, but within the pastoral idyll, they were less welcome.

Brown's work was not universally popular. Richard Page, a contemporary garden designer, wrote that he encouraged his clients to 'tear out their splendid formal gardens and replace them with his facile compositions of grass, tree clumps and rather shapeless pools and lakes', while the poet Richard Owen Cambridge joked that he aimed to die before Brown so that he could 'see heaven before it was "improved"'.

Landscape gardening couldn't be copied wholesale by the lower classes, who lacked the sheer scale of the country estates, and valued the privacy of their enclosed gardens. However, the follies, grottoes and garden nymphs were copied in miniature behind their hedges, where they were doomed to be sneered at and gradually to fall from fashion. The general rule in British garden history is that once a new style is widely adopted it becomes seen as too 'common'. This form of disparagement shows how snobbery derives primarily from the desire to set oneself apart from other people.

By the end of the eighteenth century Capability Brown's grander style was falling from favour, as people realised that it had merely replaced one kind of artificiality with another. Landscape gardening moved on from the attempt to imitate Italian pastoral landscapes, towards a more genuinely natural

The Stilt Garden at Hidcote Manor. (See pages 238–9.)

The Hidcote Tapestry Hedge. (See page 238.)

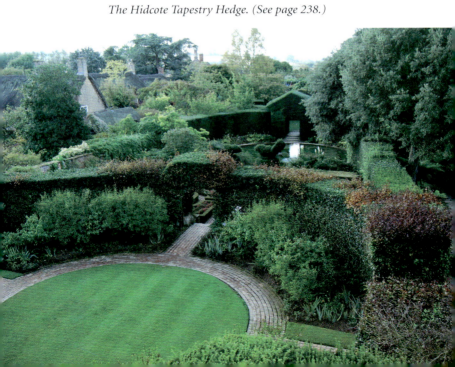

A tree being pleached at the Cotley Hunt hedgelaying competitions. (See page 276.) Note the care with which the hedgelayer lowers the tree, so as to leave it attached at the base of the trunk.

Topiary hedges at Levens Hall. (See page 174–7.)

Opposite: The Hedge Garden at Veddw House in Monmouthshire.
(See page 236.)

The Tree Cathedral near to Whipsnade was planted in the 1930s by Edmund Kell Blyth and Albert Bransom, in memory of friends lost in the First World War. It uses a mix of hedges and trees to recreate the shape of a cathedral; this is the chancel, made of white birches set against yew hedging.

Hedges as part of a formal garden design at Knebworth House in Hertfordshire.

Before and after: a hedge created in St Albans by hedgelaying volunteers.

A doorway in a beech hedge.

The maze at Hatfield House. (See pages 291–4.)

style. Many country estates did retain areas of 'parkland' but also reintroduced facsimiles of earlier styles such as box hedging and parterres. New mazes were planted, and hedged avenues returned.

The hedge, which had been temporarily in abeyance, reverted to its natural role as the backbone of garden design.

The lighter side of snobbery: the garden gnome, first imported from Germany in the 1840s by Sir Charles Isham for his rockery – he hoped they would encourage the real 'little people' to make themselves known to him. Over time they became the subject of ridicule and disdain, to the extent that they have been banned at Chelsea Flower Show since the early 1990s. In spite of the ban, Jekka McVicar's gnome Borage has illicitly visited Chelsea on several occasions – here he is hidden in the foliage.

The Cottage Garden

Since then, British gardening fashion has varied widely, without ever going back to the hedgeless 'naturalism' of Capability Brown. Subsequent garden styles have instead been defined by the ways in which they combine formal and naturalistic elements.

For instance, in the first half of the nineteenth century, garden fashion moved to the formality of the Victorian style, with carpeted bedding plants making up grand displays. But there was a swing away from that to naturalism in the 1860s and 1870s, when the gardening journalist William Robinson reacted against this style in books such as *The Wild Garden,* in which he advocated abandoning formality and using naturalistic plantings of perennials, climbers and shrubs.

William Morris had been unimpressed by the landscape gardening movement, saying:

> There is no error more prevalent in modern gardening than taking away hedges to unite many small fields into one extensive and naked lawn ... and where ground is subdivided by sunk fences,* imaginary freedom is dearly bought at the expense of actual confinement.

However he embraced Robinson's approach to naturalism, and planted the garden at the Red House (the house that Morris created and lived in and that embodied his design ethos) in an intentionally wilder style, excluding ornate bedding patterns.

---

* By 'sunk fences' he means ha-has.

This helped to popularise the 'cottage garden', which would become a mainstay of the Arts and Crafts movement.

Of course cottage gardens had simply been the patch of land that lay around the humble dwellings of the rural poor, so it is ironic that they were being reinvented by those who were a few notches up the social ladder and knew little of the limitations of the peasant lifestyle. Hunger had dictated that they were practical kitchen gardens, including a vegetable and herb patch and vines and fruit trees growing in the hedges. Fruits might include apples and pears (for cider and perry as well as the raw fruit), gooseberries and raspberries. They also tended to contain traditional hardy flowers such as foxgloves, hollyhocks, irises and daisies, as well as herbs for medicinal use.

The late nineteenth-century cottage-garden style used a similar range of plants, avoiding all hints of formality, bedding or pattern. Hedges were left to grow slightly wild, and included climbing plants and ornamental fruit trees such as crab apple or hazel. This became an increasingly popular style that would persist into the twentieth century. Gertrude Jekyll's grand garden designs used elements of the cottage-garden style. Vita Sackville-West designed one of the garden rooms at Sissinghurst as a cottage garden:

The plants grow in a jumble, flowering shrubs mingled with Roses, herbaceous plants with bulbous subjects, climbers scrambling over hedges, seedlings coming up wherever they have chosen to sow themselves.

The cottage-garden style helped fix the idea that even ordinary gardens could recreate a tiny piece of countryside. Where eighteenth-century landscape gardens had tried to mimic nature on the grand scale, the cottage garden aimed for a similar effect at a more humble level, enclosed within garden hedges. Both styles became known as the *jardin anglais,* as Europeans saw a return to nature as being characteristic of British gardening.

The Garden Palette

Centuries of changing horticultural fashion have left us with a broad palette of styles to choose from today. Around the country, you see gardens that have been influenced by formal gardens, the picturesque style, the cottage garden and Victorian bedding schemes, as well as other historic enthusiasms such as walks and avenues, the symbolic gardens of the Stuarts, rockeries, ornamental ponds and fountains, bowers and gazebos.

Whatever the style, there are few gardens that don't benefit from the enclosure and structure that hedges provide. Whether left to grow wild, rigidly clipped, used to subdivide the garden or to create shelter and privacy, they are an invaluable feature. Windows, doorways and openings can be cut into them to enhance views and provide walkways. For instance, at Ham House in London, a window in the yew hedge has been used to frame the view of a statue beyond; at Veddw House Garden in Monmouthshire the sinuous curves of the Hedge Garden create a winding pathway opening on to a pool; while at Bodnant Garden in Wales laburnum has been used to create a hedged tunnel.

A hedge doorway frames a view at Cliveden.

Hedges and interlinked trees can also be striking features in their own right. Topiary gives the gardener one obvious way of jazzing up a hedge or tree. Geometric forms can also be created by pleaching,* the process by which trees in a line are woven together and tied to form a solid shape above the ground level (the trees are sometimes grafted together as part of the process). Pleached limes and other species were

---

* Note that pleaching has a slightly different meaning for gardeners than it does when used by hedgelayers.

common in Tudor times, but fell out of fashion during the eighteenth century – more recently there has been a revival of the technique. For instance, Folly Farm, designed early in the twentieth century by Gertrude Jekyll and Edwin Lutyens, has a double row of pleached laburnums, while there is an impressive row of pleached limes in the North Garden at Sandringham.

Tapestry hedges were another early twentieth-century fashion that made the hedge a focal point rather than treating it as backdrop. They used a combination of various shades of golden and green conifers, or a mix of beech and copper beech to create a look of variegated colour. There is a fine example still in place at Hidcote Manor Garden.

Hidcote is one of the great hedge gardens of the last century. It was created by Lawrence Johnston, an American who fought for the British Army in the First World War, nearly dying in the process. Using hedges and topiaries of species including box, hornbeam, beech and yew in an extraordinary variety of ways, he divided the garden into a series of rooms. The hedges form screens, walks and backdrops to the planting displays within. Like Sissinghurst, this is a garden that displays a nice balance between formal and informal elements.*

The 'rooms' have names such as the White Garden and the Fuchsia Garden, and a spectacular variety of colour and flower schemes and water features supplement the hedged patterns. One classic feature is the famous raised hedges of the Stilt Garden. A double row of pleached hornbeams have

---

* Vita Sackville-West was a great admirer of Hidcote and used hedges to create a similar division into rooms at Sissinghurst.

been pruned so that the bare trunks support what appear to be hedges raised up over head height.

When you walk around a garden such as Hidcote you recognise the patient, devotional nature of the work that went into creating and goes into maintaining it. As you pass through the different rooms, hedges guide you and frame the open spaces. And while the flowers and plantings may have the most immediate visual impact, it is the hedges that underpin the aura of peace and permanence. It is an elegant testament to the central role they have played in the creation of the gardens of Britain.

Pleached limes in the formal garden at Knebworth.

Hemingford Grey

He that plants trees loves others besides himself.
THOMAS FULLER

As a child I read and reread Lucy Boston's Green Knowe books, which feature the adventures of various children in an ancient house where different eras intertwine. Ghostly children from long ago return to the house, and past incidents, both good and evil, haunt the present day.

Green Knowe was modelled on Lucy Boston's own house and garden, The Manor, on the Great Ouse towpath in the village of Hemingford Grey. It was built in the 1130s and has been continuously occupied ever since. It rises from the flat, misty fenland, surrounded on three sides by a moat and the slow river on the fourth.

Arriving in the location of stories that meant so much to me as a child is a strange experience. This is a garden any child would love to play in. There is a secret area surrounded by tall beech hedges, a topiary hen by the main door, as well as a few real hens clucking in a pen, and beds containing hundreds of roses. There are also numerous objects that were featured in the books, including the statue of St Christopher carrying the baby Jesus and the luxurious bamboo hedge alongside the moat, inside which Tolly, Susan, Jacob and the other children hide and play.

On the lawn there is a set of yew topiary, by the rose garden are topiary chess pieces in black and white planted squares, while to the rear of the house there is a topiary deer, the same green deer that Tolly loves so much in the books.

Lucy started to cut the pieces on the lawn in 1952, to celebrate the coronation – they were originally intended to be two

A picture of The Manor taken in 1943 by J. Oldknow (whose name Lucy borrowed for Mrs Oldknow) showing the recently planted shrubs that would become the crowns and orbs.

The crowns and orbs today.

Chess pieces foreground, crowns and orbs beyond.

pairs of crowns and two pairs of orbs. That year they weren't fully grown so she clipped them as best she could then tied in extra yew branches from the many trees in the garden. As they grew, one of the crowns seemed to want to be a different shape and she eventually cut it into a dove of peace.

Kathryn V. Graham, the American academic, has written of how children's writers use topiary 'to create an unsettling, surreal, and frightening twist on the concept of controlled yet benevolent nature under cultivation'.* She compares topiary to masks and clowns, because of the way it involves elements of disguise and falsification. I don't usually find topiary unsettling, but it can definitely sometimes be a bit weird. In

---

* *The Devil's Own Art: Topiary in Children's Fiction* – good examples are Anthony Browne's *Voices in the Park*, Elizabeth Goudge's *The Little White Horse*, Janni Howker's *The Topiary Garden* and Lemony Snicket's books.

The Children of Green Knowe, there is an example of an especially sinister topiary figure in the garden, the 'Green Noah' for which the house is named. The elderly Mrs Oldknow is letting the shape slowly grow out as legend relates the story of a gypsy's curse on the tree:

> *Snippet snappet, Shapen yew,*
> *Devil's image, Take on you.*
> *Evil grow, Evil be,*
> *Green Noah Demon tree.*

Lucy Boston based the fictional version of the St Christopher statue on one she saw at Norton Priory in Cheshire. For a recent film based on the books a replica was made in polystyrene and this is the one on display at Hemingford Grey.

Happily there is no sign of Green Noah in the garden today.

The Manor is owned by Lucy's daughter-in-law, Diana Boston. She is not at home, so my family and I are alone in the garden, keenly aware of her absence. Standing by the chess set topiary I can hear my daughter shrieking with laughter in the distance. I hear voices but I can see no one.

For a moment here we are all ghosts, invisible presences in the place that is so full of the memories of Lucy Boston and those who lived here before and after her. It is still impossible to disentangle past and present in this beautiful place, after all these centuries.

12. The Peculiar Hedges of Spitfire Island
Irregular Hedges and Hedgelike Objects

The world has not an ambition worth sharing, or a prize worth handling. Corrupt successes, disgraceful failures, or sheeplike vegetation are all it has to offer.

LOVE AMONG THE ARTISTS, GEORGE BERNARD SHAW

Spitfire Island is a busy, urban roundabout in Castle Vale, on the outskirts of Birmingham. On the central island a metal, modernist sculpture depicts the famous aircraft. The main roads are dual carriageways, with low warehouses and offices visible across the way. The homes of the area are modern, low-rise housing, with cramped front gardens.

A short walk away, there is another metal sculpture, the Castle of Vale. Gleaming in the bright sunlight, a knight on horseback rises above a castle, and a supporting cast of mythological women, possibly mermaids or angels. It combines elements of Arthurian romance with an odd, industrial feel. While I'm inspecting it a crowd of kids gather at the nearby fence of a primary school, clamouring for me to kick their ball back. It takes me three attempts, to their amusement.

What really fascinates me about Castle Vale is the range of hedges and plants on view. A few passers-by watch, looking unimpressed as I island-hop through the traffic fumes and photograph the vegetation.

Many of the front gardens have well-tended hedges, but there is also a wide variety of what I prefer to call 'hedgelike objects'. In the public areas of the housing estates, on patches of waste ground and on the traffic islands, there are shrubs and rows of small trees or bushes, clipped into the appearance of stunted hedges. They aren't formal, precise or regular enough to be called topiary, but they have been tended and prevented from taking on too wild an appearance. They have a slightly mutant look, a weirdness that perhaps arises from their juxtaposition with the urban surroundings.

Some bear a passing resemblance to Rockingham's Elephant Hedge (see pages 56–60), with its asymmetrical curves. But while that is an idiosyncratic element of a beautiful formal garden plan, these objects feel more random and uncoordinated.

On Spitfire Island itself, a fully formed hedge fringes the base of the sculpture, looking curiously pointless in the haze of the traffic fumes. On the pavement a low hedge is caged in by the railings of a pedestrian crossing. A grassy bank running up from the side of the roundabout is home to further strangely shaped shrubs, some more hedgelike than others.

I instinctively dislike hedgelike objects, but I am none the less intrigued by them. You often find them in public and municipal areas across the country: motorway service stations and supermarket car parks; the lawns in front of municipal offices and the open spaces between tower blocks; retail parks, roundabouts, petrol stations and industrial estates. On remote, bleak industrial estates you see 'hedges to no-where', perfectly formed hedges that start and then stop for no apparent reason.

And it's not just municipal authorities and corporations. In the last few days alone, I've seen a knee-high hedge shielding the bicycle shelter in a local office block, and a pub where the window boxes contained nothing but miniature hedges. Everywhere we choose to grow a few plants to relieve the concrete and brick of an urban view, we seem to have the urge to clip those plants into repressed imitations of topiary.

I struggle to articulate the reasons why I find them so ugly and irritating. It can't just be because of their awkward, uneven shapes. In Japanese gardening the art of 'cloud pruning' produces irregular shapes that could be compared to hedgelike objects, but there is a clear philosophy at work in their intentionally stylised shapes. Similarly the irregular topiary at Elvaston Castle, near Derby, and the crazy topiary of Groombridge Place's Drunken Garden, in Kent, are examples of deliberately asymmetrical design. The strange patterns of the yew hedges at Montacute in Somerset actually were an accident – the vicious winter of 1947 left one hedge weighed down by snow and twisted into new shapes. But over the following years, the gardeners tended the result, and added the same effect to an opposing hedge, giving the garden an intentionally abstract feel.*

Unlike any of these creations, a hedgelike object fails to be convincingly ornamental or to have a clear practical purpose. It seems somehow ephemeral and pointless. It is something that looks like a hedge but doesn't act like a hedge.

But why are there so many hedgelike objects? Why do we have this 'urge to clip', to create smooth surfaces for ragged

---

* Montacute is featured in the film *Sense and Sensibility* (1995), and also features a remarkable array of egg-shaped topiaries.

Hedgelike Objects: A Brief Guide

A hedge to nowhere.

Hedge failing to beautify the supermarket car park.

Strange shrubs in a retail park.

A hedge in a cage.

An anti-hedge.

Ce n'est pas un bocage.

Motorway service station greenery.

Topiary balls and litter bins.

Plastic topiary ashtray outside a pub.

bushes? Is it because hedges are such a characteristic feature of our landscape that they have become wedged in our subconscious? Somewhere deep in our psyche, is there an archetypal hedgerow shape that leaks out when we are confronted with unruly plants and a pair of secateurs?

The really surprising thing about hedgelike objects is that we are not more surprised by them. They seem completely normal. It is as though we can't allow a plant to choose its own shape. Everything must speak of human intervention, even the wild, natural elements we use for contrast with utilitarian buildings and public sites. Urban trees are often heavily pruned back by local authorities, who fear that their unchecked roots may damage nearby buildings if left unchecked. On one street where I used to live, the crab apple trees were brutally cut down, just because a few residents complained about slipping on the fruit, or having them fall on their cars.

Perhaps, deep down, we are still a bit scared of 'nature'? We like to use plants and trees for decorative purposes, but there is an ambivalence in our attitude. We allow nature to flourish, so long as we can be sure that we are still in control.

Agriculture and the later practices of gardening and landscape architecture are all ways in which we have historically taken on the forces of nature and harnessed them. Even our original construction of homes from wattle and daub was a minor victory in the battle to bend nature to our purpose. And, at a certain level, we often still seem to prefer our nature tamed – a monkey in a gilded cage rather than a wild animal on the rampage.

Orderly and Disorderly Hedges

It would be easy just to dismiss hedgelike objects as monstrosities and move on, but I think it is necessary to take a slightly more complex view. The history of Castle Vale suggests a different way of thinking about them.

Early in the last century an aerodrome was built on Castle Bromwich playing fields. The Spitfire sculpture commemorates the 12,000 aircraft built in its factory during the Second World War. In the late 1950s an overspill housing estate was created on the derelict site, with thirty-four tower blocks and an assortment of bungalows and maisonettes.

After an optimistic start, the estate fell into a decline, and by the 1970s Castle Vale was seen as one of the rougher estates in Birmingham, with drugs, graffiti, joy riding and structural problems making the news. The open spaces became bleak, uninviting places. Happily, in the 1990s, management of the estate was taken over by a Housing Action Trust, and demolition of the worst blocks began. A mixture of public investment and community action has turned the area around. Only two of the old tower blocks remain, and the low-rise blocks, which were notoriously badly built, have been replaced with the new homes that I saw.

Castle Vale's hedgelike objects are just one detail of this improvement, but they do help to soften a concrete environment with a touch of tidy greenery, and to make it clear that the area is being looked after. Today, an outsider wouldn't call the area pretty. But for those local people who came together and made a difference, the way the area looks and feels today must represent real progress.

So, while these hedgelike objects are not especially attractive, the fact that the greenery is being tended is a sign that the area is being cared for. It also shows the residents here have an investment in their community, and care enough to want to 'keep up appearances'.

Many suburban prejudices are based on how 'orderly' or 'disorderly' an area looks. Overgrown, disorderly plants and untidy hedges in front gardens, parks and green spaces are almost always seen as a sign of neglect. There are areas in many British towns where poverty and antisocial behaviour, council negligence, or a high proportion of absentee landlords lead to such symptoms. They may also feature abandoned furniture or clapped-out cars in front gardens, and boarded-up or badly maintained properties. If too many houses in an area look this way, an impression of decline is created.

This is not a new phenomenon. Back in the 1850s, the Victorian lady journalist 'Rosa' wrote about the state of contemporary rural cottages in the horticultural journal *The Cottage Gardener*. She castigates these dwellings, declaring them:

Bare, desolate and neglected; whereas for the smallest outlay, or rather without any outlay at all, those cottages might be clothed with a never-failing leafy ornament, equalling in beauty any that the most lavish expenditure could obtain ... Whenever we see a well-furnished gable of this character, a clean garden and a good boundary hedge: we may always augur well of the moral and industrial character of their possessor. These are not the sort of persons who are ever seeking parish relief.*

---

* 'Seeking parish relief' was the Victorian version of signing on the dole.

She goes on to make an even more pointed connection between appearances and inner goodness:

> There is moral beauty, too, in the cultivated cottage garden. Neatness and attendance bespeak activity, diligence, and care; neglect and untidiness tell of the BEER-HOUSE.

(I love the sense of horror she manages to convey with those capital letters.)

Today, 'good' and 'bad' estates or areas are often understood to be distinguished by such external signs. In *Estates*, Lynsey Hanley discusses the cold, uninviting nature and apparent squalor of many post-war council estates, saying that 'the privet hedges stop where the sound of shirtless men shouting begins'.

Social pressure is also a factor – in a well-tended area, those who don't 'keep up appearances' are more likely to feel pressure to conform than in an area where standards are already low. Meanwhile, to some, the well-tended front gardens of the suburbs can feel oppressive. Those who don't want to conform may choose to express their individuality through mild subversions of tradition, rather than through outright defiance and neglect.

This is probably the root of the 'competitive front garden' phenomenon in which neighbours use gnomes, pampas grass, topiary hedges and other individual touches to set themselves apart from their neighbours. These tiny rebellions against conformity allow us to express individuality at the same time as we are conforming to social expectations.

Across Britain you see streets where hedges are well tended to the point of mild sarcasm, with each front garden taking a different approach to the game of 'beat your neighbours'. Sometimes this results in ugly hedgelike objects but, perhaps because we are able to devote more time than the gardeners who tend public spaces, the results can be more aesthetically pleasing.

Hedges clipped into waves or odd curves, steps and battlements lie next door to hedges clipped into rigid humourless straight lines. There are well-ordered streets where every house has slight differences in the way they approach the care and shaping of their hedges.

Conformity to the general rule that greenery should look orderly need not mean conformity in every respect. We can still use our hedges to mark out our individuality, even when we are keeping them carefully tended.

When it comes to public areas, formal gardening is a fading tradition in Britain. The precise bedding patterns of the Victorian parks, and the municipal gardening schemes of decades such as the 1950s and 1970s now seem pedantic or dated. But those who are responsible for the upkeep of these areas know they are obliged to keep the plants 'orderly' or 'tidy'.

Time-pressed gardeners are often expected to achieve this without any more specific instruction. Tidiness is a subjective concept, but in general something that looks like a man-made object with smooth surfaces seems tidier than the wild forms of nature. Sometimes the result is a kind of improvised topiary, but more often the gardeners just compress the shrubs into the weird, awkward shapes of hedgelike objects.

So, the one and only virtue of these objects is that the gardeners have taken a potentially untidy piece of nature and made it orderly. Without this intervention, the plants would

Hedge wars.

be in danger of looking neglected, and the area might start to look rundown.

However, they achieve this in a manner that lacks patience and real engagement. Like the architectural pastiches of the out-of-town supermarkets they often accompany, hedge-like objects make a superficial nod to the past, without truly reflecting the tradition they are imitating. They are quick fixes, closer to the prefab classrooms, badly planned tower blocks and shoddy modern shopping centres that blighted the country in the last century.

On the whole, I don't think it would be a great loss if they eventually followed the worst of the prefabs and tower blocks into the oblivion of history.

The Whale-Shaped Hedge

It must at least be confessed that to embellish the
form of nature is an innocent amusement.
LIVES OF THE POETS, SAMUEL JOHNSON

In the late 1990s, Zac Monroe had the most beautiful
hedge in Brixton. He had clipped the shrubs at the front
of his house into a whale. It even had a blow-hole shooting
water towards the sky, in the form of a white-flowering plant
fanning out at its peak. To complete the picture, neighbours
had planted clematis that was climbing up the phone wires
beside the whale.

You would expect the local council to appreciate residents
making such an effort to decorate their street. In fact Lambeth
Council decreed that Zac's hedge must be cut down. Their
excuse was that it was obstructing the pavement, but you can't
help but suspect that they just wanted to squash a moment of
creative individualism and impose their vision of conformity.

Zac campaigned against the decision and got the news-
papers and the BBC round to view his masterpiece. One of his
main irritations was that it was the council's job to keep the
street furniture in good condition and instead they concerned
themselves with trying to block his contribution to the neighbourhood. 'We were just trying to beautify our street,' he said.
'And to fight for our right to stop Lambeth destroying that.'
He ultimately lost the battle to save his hedge but at least

succeeded in drawing attention to the joyless pen-pushing of the council along the way.

I recently talked to Zac, who is an architect. From a professional viewpoint, he sees greenery as a natural element that helps to soften the urban environment of concrete and brick. He feels that urban gardening will always have an element of artifice, simply because towns are not a 'natural' environment. But when you clip plants into topiary it is a way of making this artifice more self-evident – so urban topiary can be knowingly absurd and self-deprecating at the same time. And it is also a genuine way of bringing a bit of self-expression and creativity to our streets.

If anything, I think we should have more whale-shaped hedges. Imagine how beautiful our towns and cities could be if every street had at least one hedge clipped into an ambitious topiary – elephants, towers, steam engines and dinosaurs in green, and flowers climbing up all the lamp-posts and telegraph poles. There are different ways this could be achieved. In Zac's case the council was the obstacle, but it needn't be this way. The town of Railton in Tasmania has declared itself to be a 'town of topiary' and both the public and private gardens contain fine specimens ranging from a dodo to a spider to a Tasmanian tiger. There is no reason why British councils couldn't emulate this example.

Alternatively, individuals can take ownership of, and pride in, their immediate locations by other means. My friend Eryl has, through extended lobbying, managed to pressure her local council into creating an urban meadow on a previously disused patch of ground, and providing planters for use of the residents of her tower block. Meanwhile guerrilla gardeners have often achieved success by planting first and negotiating with the landowner afterwards. Recent examples include the planting of flowers in potholes and the creation of a lavender hedge on a traffic island in South London. While councils and landowners may object, and would often deny permission for such work if it were sought, they may accept it as a creative improvement to the environment once it is a fait accompli.

I already regard well-clipped hedges as minor works of art, expressing the personality of each resident of an area. But today's hedges tend to be fairly restrained, and there is less topiary than there was a few decades ago. There are signs that topiary is making a gradual comeback. Within a couple of miles of me there is a green bird taking flight above an otherwise ordinary box hedge, and a topiary cat waiting to pounce on a topiary mouse.

However, we still need more exuberance, more spectacular subjects. We need guerrilla gardeners, far-sighted councils and individual enthusiasts to reshape the nondescript hedge-like objects of municipal spaces into fantastical shapes. We need to take back the urban environment and make it a beautiful place. Every new topiary hedge would be a blow in the battle against conformity. And all anyone out there needs to help make this vision real is a pair of garden clippers, and a bit of imagination.

People of Britain – the future of our hedges is in your hands.

13. The Rural Idyll
Preserving the Countryside

They found themselves standing on the very edge of the
Wild Wood. Rocks and brambles and tree-roots behind them,
confusingly heaped and tangled; in front a great space of
quiet fields, hemmed by lines of hedges black on the snow ...
THE WIND IN THE WILLOWS, KENNETH GRAHAME

As I travel through Britain I am constantly struck by how glorious the landscape is, and by the beauty and variety of its hedge-fringed lanes. Dog roses, holly and ivy, climbing plants and flowering shrubs intermingle with the hedgerows to create a mosaic of different shades and shapes. The hedges are monuments to times long past, preserving the indigenous plants that would once have grown wild here. Today, we feel a need to protect these hedges and the countryside in general, for environmental reasons and to prevent rural beauty being lost to posterity. But this wasn't always the case.

In the early nineteenth century, William Cobbett wrote of the glory of the countryside in *Rural Rides*:

The hedges are now full of the shepherd's rose, honey-suckles, and all sorts of wild flowers; so that you are upon a grass walk, with this most beautiful of all flower gardens and shrubberies on your one hand, and with the corn on the other. And as thus you go from field to field (on foot or on horseback), the sort of corn, the sort of underwood and timber, the shape and size of the fields, the height of the hedge-rows, the height of the trees, all continually varying. Talk of pleasure-ground indeed!

However, much as Cobbett appreciated the views, his main focus was not on rural preservation: instead he was campaigning on issues such as bad landlords, rotten boroughs, rural poverty and the unfairness of the game laws. It would not have occurred to him to worry about the future survival of the hedgerows he was riding past.

Historic attitudes to the countryside across the centuries were complex and varied, but generally focused on issues other than conservation. Rural depopulation and deprivation were common concerns. In the Saxon and Norman periods intensive manual farming had supported a reasonably dense rural population. Later developments from the wool industry and enclosures to the loss of cottage industries in the early industrial period led to a constant drift of population from the country to the city, and poverty among those who stayed behind.

The increasing mobility of the population also led to concerns about vagrancy. After the Black Death killed between a third and a half of the population in the mid-fourteenth century, scarce agricultural workers were able to travel to the job paying the best wages, and this gave them a new degree of freedom. Later on, less fortunate wandering labourers often became homeless, and much political will was devoted to the problem of vagrants – in the enclosures period when many rural workers became homeless, workhouses were created as a 'solution' to the problem.

It was really only in the last couple of centuries that conservation of the landscape itself became a popular cause – and only in the last fifty years or so that hedgerows became a priority within that cause.

Rural hedgerow in Leicestershire.

Idealising the Countryside

We are now more focused on rural preservation, but we have perhaps developed a tendency to see the countryside through rose-tinted glasses. John Major bowdlerised an Orwell quotation in his description of Britain:*

> The country of long shadows on cricket grounds, warm beer, invincible green suburbs, dog lovers and pools fillers and, as George Orwell said, 'Old maids bicycling to holy communion through the morning mist'.

There was a similarly nostalgic undercurrent in Tolkien's description of the Shire, a warm, simple rural place which contrasts with the proto-industrial horrors of the harsher world beyond. Over the last century, this kind of vision of Britain has become widespread – with the countryside and the village being used as a cosy definition of 'authentic Britishness'.

The romanticisation of the countryside first started to gather pace in the eighteenth century. The landscape gardeners treated the rural scene as aesthetically pleasing, trying to recreate it in their gardens, and to bring down the barriers between the garden and the country. Artists and writers helped to cement this view. By the early part of the nineteenth century,

---

* The original quote, from *England Your England*, is grittier, also speaking of 'The clatter of clogs in the Lancashire mill towns, the to and fro of the lorries on the Great North Road, the queues outside the labour exchanges, the rattle of pin-tables in the Soho pubs.'

landscape painting was becoming more naturalistic, as for instance in John Constable's paintings of Suffolk. Wordsworth not only recorded his extensive walks in the country, but also wrote poems that rhapsodised about its beauty. The Romantics depicted the country as a pure, emotionally authentic counterpart to the coldly logical, industrialised city.

The idea of 'tourism' in rural Britain also started to become fashionable. In the 1780s, William Gilpin wrote about the 'picturesque beauty' of the English landscape, and challenged the notion that the Grand Tour of the continent was the best way to gain aesthetic inspiration. He spoke up for an artistic appreciation of non-classical artistic objects such as decaying ruins and even the rural poor of the countryside (who were no doubt delighted to be the distant object of his condescending fascination). Tourists started to flock to Wordsworth's beloved Lake District to sketch the landscape.

This romanticisation wasn't restricted to the idle rich. In the lives of ordinary people at this stage there was a powerful reason for rural nostalgia. The poverty that Cobbett observed in *Rural Rides* was driving more and more people out of the country into the embrace of urban life. The newly enclosed fields were farmed on an increasingly industrial scale and there were fewer smallholdings and rural jobs. As people moved to new urban areas they naturally looked back on their previous homes as a paradise lost.

(Family legend tells of my wife's great-grandmother arriving in England early last century. The family's horse-rearing business in the Wicklow mountains had been destroyed by the dawn of the motor car and they were forced to emigrate. When she arrived in Rochdale, on a boat travelling up the canal from Manchester, she burst into tears as soon as she set eyes on the satanic mills and smoky red brick walls of her new home town.)

Over the course of a century or so a huge proportion of the population went from a rural existence to an urban one, and heard tales from their elders of the life that they had left behind. So fear of the countryside and the memory of the hard labour of agricultural life were gradually transformed into a sentimental attachment to country life.

This influenced a broad sweep of popular culture. The Arts and Crafts movement harked back to the hand-made techniques of cottage industry, the folk music revival emphasised the authenticity of old rural songs (as opposed to the commercialism of music halls) and traditions such as morris dancing and the maypole came to be seen as the last remnants of 'Merrie England'.

In the same period, walking in the countryside became a popular leisure activity for urban dwellers. The craze for picturesque tourism was one factor. Another was the development of cheap transport, first the railways, then the buses and cars of the twentieth century, which allowed easier access to the countryside.

In crowded, polluted cities such as Manchester, Liverpool and Glasgow, those who could afford to get out of the city for the day started to visit the mountains and fells that surrounded them for the exercise and a change of scenery. As the countryside was used more as a leisure destination, attitudes towards it were transformed. While the amount of common land had already been greatly reduced, many ancient rights of way had survived. Walkers were passing between the hedges of ancient green lanes and climbing the stiles and gates that had previously been used by the locals. Rambling gave people a feeling of ownership of the countryside, even if they didn't live there, and focused attention on the idea that the landscape was part of our national heritage, something we should protect and preserve.

Protecting Rural Britain

The political movement to protect open spaces and the countryside intensified in the second half of the nineteenth century, as the cities became more crowded. Many great urban parks date from this period, green areas preserved in the cities by those concerned for the welfare and health of the poor. For instance Leeds' impressive Roundhay Park was bought by Leeds City Council for £139,000 in 1871 and given to the people of Leeds, while Waterlow Park in North London was donated by the philanthropist Sir Sydney Waterlow in 1889 as 'a garden for the gardenless'.

The Commons Preservation Society (now called the Open Spaces Society) was set up in 1865, to protect rural and urban common land. (Many towns had their commons enclosed and built over in the eighteenth and nineteenth centuries, including Birmingham and Oldham.) In 1893 the Society for Checking the Abuses of Public Advertising started campaigning against commercial hoardings in the countryside (a great bugbear of the period), and in 1895 the National Trust was founded by a group of slightly eccentric philanthropists,

Octavia Hill, Robert Hunter and Hardwicke Rawnsley, to protect threatened buildings and landscape areas.*

The inheritors of country houses and estates were allowed to donate their property to the Trust in lieu of death duties for much of the last century – often with an arrangement for the family to continue to live in part of the property. This is the source of many of the country houses and classic gardens now open to the public. The various National Trust Acts have granted the Trust the power to declare land inalienable, meaning it can't be sold without special parliamentary permission.

The Trust now owns huge parts of the country – a recent list gives the top three UK landowners as the Forestry Commission, the royal family, and the National Trust in third place.†　While it is often criticised for imposing a rather nostalgic, fusty view of British heritage, it has clearly had a huge impact on how we define that heritage.

By the twentieth century, the importance of rural landscapes was well established. For instance the preservationist Vaughan Cornish described lowland village England as an arcadia, writing that 'the unspoilt parts of agricultural England have a beauty which is unique in the scenery of civilisation'. The Council for the Preservation of Rural England was formed in 1926, the brainchild of the architect and preservationist

---

* In the 1930s the Trust received an especially bizarre series of donations from 'Ferguson's Gang', a secretive group of masked ladies with cockney accents – apparently they were wealthy young women in disguise, inspired by the Clough Williams-Ellis book *England and the Octopus*, and its denunciation of urban sprawl.

† Land occupied by: Forestry Commission, 2,400,000 acres; royal family (including Crown Estates, Duchy of Cornwall etc), 677,000 acres; National Trust, 630,000 acres; Ministry of Defence, 592,000 acres.

Sir Patrick Abercrombie. It campaigned against urban sprawl and ribbon development (that is, urban growth spreading alongside roads).

However, rural hedgerows were not a priority for the CPRE at first. In 1933 Abercrombie was actually defending their destruction, writing that 'there are certainly parts of England whose landscapes will be improved by a greater landscape of sweeps of open, highly cropped fields: a new scale may be added to what in some places is a monotonous iteration of hedge and hedgerow tree.'

These early preservationists had an unfortunately elitist bent. They argued for more paternalistic control of planning, and contrasted the virtues of the past, where a few landowners had great power, with what they saw as the laissez-faire anarchy of modernity. For instance Abercrombie wrote:

> If the country had remained in the hands of the same families who have done so much to create its typical English Beauty in the past ... the greater use of the country ... might have been directed into more defined areas.

This led them to mistrust suburbia, which was seen as a sham rural existence. Those little boxes with their hedged garden and front yard were seen as wasting land that could have been saved for the countryside, or turned into higher density housing. The fact that most British people wanted a garden and a small piece of land around their home was of no consequence when compared to the importance of preserving the rural idyll.

The preservationists were not always in favour of the traditional over the modern. Some subscribed to the new ideas of Le Corbusier, imagining autobahn-style motorways linking high-rise, high-density future cities whose populations would be happily housed in towers, while the countryside remained virgin. You can't help wondering whether they wanted to preserve the landscape for the people of Britain – or save it from the people of Britain. There was disdain in contemporary literature for any sighting of groups of 'cockneys' (used as a generic term for the urban poor) or motor-picnickers in charabancs. Abercrombie complained of the pervasiveness of dissonant sounds such as car horns and gramophones in the countryside, while the open-air enthusiast Cyril Joad lamented the fact that in parts of the Lake District the 'atmosphere vibrates to the sounds of negroid music. Girls with men are jazzing to gramophones in meadows.'

Comically dated as these attitudes appear, they express a deeper unease about the mixing of urban and rural. From the start, the CPRE showed signs of the 'Not In My Back Yard' mentality to rural protection. They also campaigned strongly for the creation of green belts, which were adopted by various cities from 1935 onwards.

Green belts and planning restrictions have helped to preserve rural areas from being absorbed into cities. But they can also create problems – for instance the focus on 'brown-field' development in recent years actually led to a lot of building over urban playing fields and back gardens (both of which have been treated as 'brownfield'). Meanwhile in rural areas the resulting lack of new homebuilding leads to shortages of affordable housing.

Thankfully, at least when it comes to hedges, the CPRE has become far more enlightened. From the 1960s onwards its members have campaigned to protect hedgerows. Recently

Bill Bryson became president and in his inaugural speech made a heartfelt plea for them:

> I am really worried about hedgerows. They are what define the English landscape and everywhere they are just quietly fading away. Hedgerows die bit by bit, as here. Eventually you end up with no hedgerows at all – and this is the fate that I fear is awaiting very large swathes of the countryside.

Rights of Way

Today, we take the ability to walk through the countryside on public footpaths, through open spaces and along rights of way for granted. In fact, many of these would have been lost to us if it hadn't been for historic campaigns to preserve them. As the enclosure hedges turned common land into privately owned land, legislation in 1815 allowed landowners to block footpaths and revoke rights of way, preventing access to ancient common land that had escaped the clutches of the enclosures.

Various societies were created for the protection of local footpaths (two of the earliest were in York and Manchester). In addition, ramblers' groups started to spring up, finally joining together into the National Council of Ramblers' Federations (which is now the Ramblers' Assocation).

One of the most iconic moments in the struggle for countryside access came when a group of young ramblers from Manchester organised a mass trespass on Kinder Scout, on 24 April 1932. This part of the Derbyshire Peaks was closed to the public, and the protest was a response to a previous run-in they'd had with armed gamekeepers.

A rowdy, high-spirited group of several hundred ramblers managed to outwit the police and gamekeepers and reach the peak of Kinder. There were numerous arrests and five people were imprisoned for sentences of up to six months. The protest was initially opposed by the official ramblers' groups as being too radical, and demonised in the press as a communist stunt. However, the harsh punishment meted out to the ramblers touched a chord, and the public mood turned increasingly in favour of countryside access.

Several major achievements followed in the post-war years. The National Parks and Access to the Countryside Act became law in December 1949, and created the machinery for all footpaths to be surveyed and mapped. Eventually the Ramblers' Association managed to persuade the Ordnance Survey to include these on all maps, meaning that for the first time there was a permanent record of our collective rights of way across the countryside, a huge step in the protection of these paths. In 1968 the Countryside Act forced local councils to take this further and signpost footpaths, reinforcing the idea that the paths belonged to everyone.

This is a long slow battle. Kinder Scout was only opened up to the public in the 1950s while much of the rest of the Peak District remained closed. The Right to Roam legislation introduced in 2000 was a step in the right direction, but implementation of it has been painfully slow. However, the basic principle has been established, hopefully beyond doubt, that the people of this country have a right to access to the countryside and that ancient rights of way should be protected wherever possible.

One recent case in which these rights were tested was the thirteen-year legal fight between the Ramblers' Association and millionaire landlord Nicholas van Hoogstraten over the footpath across his land. He despised ramblers and had blocked access using a gate, barbed wire, refrigeration units and even a newly built barn. The fact that you can now, in theory, walk along the hedgerows from Framfield to Honey's Green in East Sussex is testament to the tenacity of the Ramblers' Association in defending our rights of way.

The Village Green Preservation Society

I'm in Sambourne, the winner of the 2009 Warwickshire Best Kept Village competition. It is a disarmingly beautiful and bucolic place – I walk past Tudor-style white and black timber-framed cottages, thatched roofs, well-tended hedges and beautiful gardens around a small village green. The Green Dragon pub is bedecked in flower baskets and greenery. Inside I raise a glass in an ironic but affectionate toast to 'Merrie England'.

The CPRE has run these competitions around the country since the 1930s. The loss of so many young men, so many gardeners, hedgelayers and labourers in the Great War had led to a decline in the condition of many villages and the countryside around them. In some areas the art of hedgelaying was only kept alive by a few old souls who hadn't fought in the war and continued to train up younger apprentices. For instance many of the inter-war generation of Cotswold hedgelayers learnt their art from one man called Sykes, who was brought in from outside the area specifically for this purpose.

In an attempt to reverse the deterioration of rural areas, the Best Kept Village competitions were established. The rules specifically include the condition of the village's hedges. In the ten-point checklist used by judges, item three concerns the 'condition of public and private buildings, gardens and allotments, including hedges, walls, fences and outhouses'.

The competitions are a charming institution, but they illustrate some of the complexities of conservation. The whole idea of the 'perfect village' is a recent one. Sambourne has been in existence since the eighth century, but it is unlikely that in centuries past it would have satisfied any of the demands of the Best Kept Village judges.

The wider danger is that, instead of conserving the real countryside, we could end up aspiring towards a Disney-fied version of it, and forgetting about more practical rural concerns. In the wider countryside, it is the practical issues that will dictate the future of our hedges, not aesthetic guidelines.

The contemporary image and upkeep of country villages is partly down to gentrification and to people with an urban or suburban mindset using them as a refuge from city stress. From the cottage garden and the green belt to nimbyism, second-homers, the CPRE and the National Trust, there has been a tendency to see the countryside as authentically British and to idealise it. On the positive side, this has helped to save hedgerows, paths, woods, heaths and parks that might otherwise have been lost. But an overly sanitised view of rural life can also become an obstacle to sustainable preservation.

The real countryside was created by those who worked the land, by the farmers, drovers, traders, hedgelayers, stone wall builders and ditch diggers. Today, many rural Britons feel aggrieved by a combination of neglect by city-centric governments and demands placed on them by planners and campaigners who do not understand their way of life. While much of the interference is done with good intentions, it is possible that the pendulum has swung too far towards an over-regulated, over-fussy approach to conservation.

For instance, when it comes to trees and hedges, there are so many detailed rules and regulations that local people and farmers can become reluctant to cut anything down, and we end up with overgrown hedgerows rather than sensible maintenance by those who know the area best.

This leads to an ongoing loss of hedgerow trees – when they become overgrown, councils often use health and safety as an excuse for felling them. (Jon Stokes of the Tree Council has pointed me towards research by the National Tree Safety Group that suggests the risk posed by roadside trees is minuscule, but this risk is none the less often the reason given for the removal of these trees, and the consequent loss of biodiversity.)

To protect our hedgerows, we need to focus on the reasons why they were tended in the first place. For a start, they were created in a landscape where livestock farming was ubiquitous. Today, livestock farmers face many problems. The foot and mouth outbreak, bovine TB, and supermarkets sourcing cheap meat abroad have combined to make livestock farming increasingly unprofitable – but it is such farmers who have the most pressing need to maintain hedges. The more land is converted to arable, the more hedgerows we will lose.

It is also worth considering the relationship between foxhunting and hedgerows. Whilst all sorts of people participate, hunting has often been associated with the wealthier classes. In the nineteenth century, the Berkeley Hunt was able to hunt (in its distinctive yellow jackets) all the way from Berkeley Castle near Gloucester to Berkeley Square in London, such was the extent of the land owned by the Berkeley and fitz Hardinge families, ownership that dated from the Conquest.

Many people find the symbolism or practice of foxhunting distasteful – as a typical town-dweller, I'm a bit squeamish about it myself. But the hunts have been among the great protectors of hedgerows. Some, such as the Cottesmore Hunt in Rutland and the Cotley Hunt in Somerset, regularly organise hedgelaying competitions. There is a natural symbiosis between hunting and hedges. For the hunters, well-kept hedgerows open up the countryside, while overgrown ones are barriers. Hedgelayers using the Midland style (and other styles with exposed stakes) traditionally cut the tops of the hedge stakes at an angle upwards towards the hedge so they won't injure horses who jump the hedge and could get snagged on a stake cut differently.

The preservation of hedgerows and the countryside is an important issue but, as its history shows, it is also a complex one. We need to continue to protect common land and rights of access, and to try to protect rural beauty and biodiversity. However, the landscape is not best served by seeing it as a theme park or museum for tourists and second-homers.

Instead, we need a living, breathing countryside where people live and work the land. Hedgerows are most likely to survive in that countryside if they are tended because of the important roles they play, not just because we value them as symbols of bucolic simplicity.

The Hedgerows of Eaglescairnie Mains

Dumb is the hedge where the crabs hang yellow
Bright as the blossoms of spring
THE STORY OF THE GLITTERING PLAIN, WILLIAM MORRIS

One examplar of good practice in hedgerow maintenance is the family farm at Eaglescairnie Mains in East Lothian, run by Michael and Barbara Williams. Michael is a strong advocate of 'sympathetic farming'. This means he aims to unite landscape and wildlife conservation with profitable agriculture. As the Lothians' Farming and Wildlife Advisory Group Demonstration Farm he receives many visits from local farmers, students and school parties who want to see the benefits of integrating farming and conservation at close quarters.

One of the newer hedges was planted twelve years ago along the path of an old fenceline. It is 70 per cent hawthorn but also includes blackthorn, guelder rose, and hazel. On the hedge margins, sunflowers and a variety of other wildflowers are planted, all selected for their appeal to birds. A variety of plant species provides berries, grains and kale for birds to eat (Michael refers to the mix as a kind of 'muesli for birds').

Bees are also catered for. The nectar crops which are crucial for bees are often lost to intensive farming processes, whereas Michael makes sure to encourage them. Bees aren't just important for conservation reasons – pollination of many crops is improved by a healthy bee population.

The hedge serves an additional purpose in creating a wildlife corridor. Before it was planted, the fields at this point were wide open. By creating linear cover and a link between areas of woodland, the hedgerow provides protection for animal life and a hawking route for bats. The dead wood and plant litter inside it provide a habitat for many invertebrates and this in turn brings the bats, and other predators such as shrews and birds.

It is notable how much land Michael leaves between the hedgerow and the point at which he starts to plough the field. A lot of farmers plough right up to the hedge, but leaving a wider margin is a great encouragement to birds and other wildlife. There are particularly active populations of yellowhammers, goldfinches and chaffinches as well as a variety of other species.

One of the traditional virtues of a tightly laid hedge is that it allows sufficient room for small birds to go 'inside' the hedge, whilst denying access to predators such as buzzards, magpies and sparrowhawks. Roger Parris, a champion West Country hedgelayer, says that a hedge should be laid 'thick enough so that a butterfly can fly in – but not through', which will also leave enough room for the hedge to breathe.

Michael also tends and revitalises the ancient hedges that were on his land when he arrived. The oldest is known to be about two centuries old. This is confirmed both from the number of species it contains and by local maps that verify its existence in the early nineteenth century.

Eaglescairnie Mains is one of many examples of how good hedge care can also help to protect the ecosystems of the countryside, and how thoughtful farming practice and rural conservation can mutually reinforce one another.

14. The Hedge People
The Symbolism and Politics of Hedges

The boys and girls play in the ditches till they go to
school, and they play in the hedges and ditches every
hour they can get out of school, and the moment their
time is up they go to work among the hedges and ditches,
and though they may have had to read standard authors
at school, no sooner do they get among the furrows
than they talk hedge and ditch language.

FIELD AND HEDGEROW, RICHARD JEFFERIES

Given the many ways in which hedges are entwined with the story of Britain, it is no surprise to find that they have often been used as symbolic objects in folk tales and other stories.

Hedges often create impassable obstacles, as in the early English tale 'The Princess of Colchester',* where the princess must tap a hedge with her wand three times and say 'Pray, hedge, let me come through,' before she can continue on her magical journey. In the story of 'St Godric and the Hunted Stag', a well-nigh impenetrable brushwood of thorns and

---

* Included in *English Fairy Tales* by Joseph Jacob as 'The Three Heads of the Well'. This collection also includes 'Nix Naught Nothing'.

briars protects a stag from the hunting party that is pursuing it. (St Godric subsequently offers the stag protection after the hunters manage to laboriously cut through the hedge.)

In the original European version of the Baba Yaga story, a comb is thrown down that turns into a forest. In an English version of the story, Nix Naught Nothing is fleeing from a magician, along with the magician's daughter who uses the same trick and 'lo and behold! out of every one of the comb-prongs there sprang up a prickly briar, which grew so fast that the Magician found himself in the middle of a thorn hedge!'

Tolkien couldn't resist bringing hedges into the mythology of Middle Earth. When the Fellowship of the Ring leave the Shire, they pass the Hedge, also known as the High Hay, a great hedge grown as a defence against the monsters of the Old Forest. The Hedge is 'unclimbed and unclimbable' (which sounds somewhat like an early version of leylandii).

The use of hedges as a barrier is mocked in another British tale, 'Of Hedging a Cuckoo', wherein the traditionally clueless men of Gotham hope to keep a cuckoo to sing to them all year round.

And in the midst of their town they made a hedge round in compass and they got a Cuckoo, and put her into it, and said, 'Sing there all through the year, or thou shalt have neither meat nor water.' The Cuckoo, as soon as she perceived herself within the hedge, flew away. 'A vengeance on her!' said they. 'We did not make our hedge high enough.'*

---

* 'Of Hedging a Cuckoo' and 'Yallery Brown' are included in *More English Fairy Tales* by Joseph Jacobs.

Hedges also appear in folk tales as a border or gateway. There are numerous tales in which fairies and elves emerge from the hedgerows to aid or curse the protagonists. In the Irish tale 'The Fairy Tree of Dooros', the fairies dance so much they wear out their shoes and 'for a whole week after the leprechauns, the fairies' shoemakers, were working night and day making new ones, and the rip, rap, tap, tap of their little hammers were heard in all the hedgerows'.* In the tale 'Yallery Brown', the hero Tom meets a bogle, a sinister little creature, at the base of a hedge. Even that modern hero Harry Potter first encounters Dobby the elf watching him from the garden hedge.

The word 'hag', referring to a witch-like figure, is probably derived from 'haga'. It is speculated that a hag was able to 'hedge-ride', or cross the boundary of the civilised settlements into the wild forest and return unscathed, which some took to mean that they were in league with dark forces beyond (although they were probably just wise old women). The rural superstition survives that you can foil witches by leaving holly trees growing in your hedges – because hags or witches are supposed to be repelled by holly.

For the most part, staying within our hedges is regarded as the safe, secure option – with wilderness and danger lying beyond. But the hedge as a border is not always a sinister motif. Sometimes, as with Alice's rabbit hole, a hedge is the gateway to a magical world. In Robin McKinley's folk tales a door in the hedge leads to the land of the fairies, while E. M. Forster wrote a short story called 'The Other Side of the

---

* *Irish Fairy Tales*, Edmund Leamy

Hedge' in which the protagonist goes through the hedge to an alternative reality. In Philip Pullman's *Amber Spyglass,* the hero Will also finds his first window to another world hidden on the patch of grass beside the bushes of a garden hedge.

Hedges are so ubiquitous in Britain, they have evidently become wedged in our subconscious, helping to frame these stories of barriers, doorways and journeys. In psychological terms, they seem to represent our need to feel safe in our own space. We build ourselves a hedge, then gather everything and everyone we love and feel safe with inside the hedge. But occasionally we wonder what lies on the outside, and dream of magical escapes to the other side.

This links to our ideas of 'self' and 'other', 'insider' and 'outsider'. We include some aspects of the world in our enclosed safety zone, and place wilder or more confusing aspects of the world beyond, in the 'other'. And just as woodland ghosts preserve a small piece of the ancient forest, so too does the hedgerow retain a hint of the unknown fears that the forest once held for us.

The Hedge People

Hedges have also been used as symbols of the ordinary, common people, as opposed to the ruling class. For instance, Richard Jefferies referred to the English labourer as 'the man of the hedges'. This connects to a linguistic usage that was common from the sixteenth century onwards: 'hedge' used as a prefix referred to something humble, or of the lowest class – from the contemptuous usage of 'plying one's trade under a hedge'. So in the countryside you would find hedge-doctors, hedge-lawyers and even hedge-wenches, and someone of a lowly background could be described as hedge-born or 'born under a hedge'.*

There were hedge schools too: during the Protestant Ascendancy in Ireland, in the late seventeenth and eighteenth centuries, the Penal Laws imposed many injustices on Catholics, such as the ban on owning horses that were worth more than £5. Catholics were debarred from inheriting land previously owned by Protestants, and were refused primogeniture – their estates had to be divided between the sons rather than passing to the eldest child, which meant that land holdings of individual Catholics gradually became smaller. (Primogeniture concentrates wealth and power – by removing it the lawmakers aimed to prevent individual Catholics from becoming too rich.)

The Penal Laws also specified that 'no person of the popish religion shall publicly or in private houses teach school, or instruct youth in learning within this realm'. One reason the Gaelic language survived (in spite of attempts to convert the population to speaking English) was the hedge-schools. Both the language and knowledge of Catholic culture were maintained by hedge-priests and hedge-masters teaching in secrecy. Initially these schools were hidden in fields and ditches behind the cover of the hedgerows. Once the Penal Laws were repealed in 1784, they continued to operate in barns, cowhouses, mud cabins or schoolhouses built of sods. John O'Hagan described them:

---

* 'Who will swear the hobs and boggarts who live in the hedges and in hollow trees and the wild men who hide in the woods?' Hilary Mantel, *Wolf Hall*

... still crouching 'neath the sheltering hedge,
Or stretched on mountain fern
The teacher and his pupils met
Feloniously to learn.

To 'hedge' also means to 'evade', as a countryside full of hedgerows acted as a kind of maze through which 'low types' from poachers and thieves to rabble-rousers could evade pursuers. In the early nineteenth-century uprisings of the Luddites and the Swing Riots, in which rural workers gathered to destroy the machinery that was undertaking their labour, the protesters were often able to melt away undetected into the countryside they knew so well.

Hedges were more than a hiding place for the poor. They were also a source of sustenance, which was crucial as common land continued to be removed by enclosure. Fruit and nut trees found in hedges included crab apple, damson, wild cherry, hazel and pear.* Flowers and fruits were used as flavourings and to make drinks such as blackberry or elderberry wine, sloe gin, cider and perry. Those with the knowhow could find birds and their eggs, small mammals, twigs and coppiced stakes of wood in the hedgerows. As the forests shrunk, wood became scarce, and a new crime of hedge-breaking, taking wood for fuel from hedges, came into being. (Interestingly, the Tree Council recently stressed that with the

---

* The hedges near the Stiperstones in Shropshire are exceptions to Hooper's Law because squatters and free miners of the eighteenth and nineteenth century planted such a variety of domestically useful trees in their smallholdings' hedges, including gooseberry, spindle and laburnum (probably for the wood).

increasing need for sustainable energy hedgerow trees might again become important as a local source of firewood and for growing fruit.)

I always find it strange when 'common' is used as a derogatory term. At root, it simply means 'shared by all'. I suppose that, in a classbound society, the fact that many people share something means it has no status or 'exclusiveness' and is therefore despised by those who see themselves as being better than the common people.

Across the centuries, hedgerows have been a refuge, a hiding place and a source of food, just as common land was in the past. Since 'hedge' as an adjective or prefix has lost the derogatory overtones that 'common' still retains, maybe it would make more sense today to refer to 'the common people' as 'the hedge people' instead?

Hedge Funds and Financial Crises

From meaning 'dodge' or 'evade', to hedge also came to mean 'to insure oneself against, or avoid, loss', as in 'hedging your bets'. This is how 'hedge funds' got their name. Hedge funds are means by which fund managers gamble with the money of wealthy individuals. Hedge funds use investment strategies with a high probability of profit by attempting to hedge some of the risk using methods such as short selling and derivatives trading. Like investment bankers they also use high leveraging (borrowing money to fund an investment or bet) in order to increase their potential gains. Leveraging makes it possible to lose more money than you started out with. For instance, when you buy a house with a mortgage and a £10,000 deposit,

Hedgerow Jelly

A wide variety of food can be found in hedges, including bilberries, cloudberries, common mallow, dandelions, hedge garlic, horseradish, pignuts, nettles, sloes, sweet chestnuts, water mint and wild cherries. Children today still experience the fun of searching for hedgerow food, if only through the annual blackberrying of the late summer, which leaves them with scratched arms, fingers stained blue and (hopefully) enough fruit for jam, crumble and pies. If you want to try your own foraging, here is a slightly more ambitious recipe, for Hedgerow Jelly.

This recipe makes a moderate amount of jelly – you will not need more than half a dozen jars, which need to be sterilised by heating in a medium oven for 15 minutes. Fruits that may be used are blackberries, elderberries, hawthorn berries, rose hips, rowan berries, and crab apples or cooking apples, which are necessary for the pectin that makes the jelly set. Haws and rowan berries take longer to soften.

1lb roughly chopped crab apples (or windfalls/ cooking apples)
1lb other mixed hedgerow fruit, stems/leaves removed
Juice of a small lemon
Granulated sugar – probably around 3lb, maybe more, maybe less – see below

You will also need a heavy-bottomed saucepan, a large bowl, a jelly bag or a sieve lined with muslin, and a measuring jug, a saucer (cooled in the freezer), and enough covers or lids for the jam jars.

1. Wash and quickly drain the fruit.
2. Put the fruit in the pan and add enough cold water to cover it. Bring to the boil and simmer gently till the fruit is soft.
3. Strain overnight in the jelly bag, or through muslin layers in a sieve, and don't squeeze/press the fruit to hurry the process or you will get a cloudy jelly.
4. Measure the resulting juice into the cleaned pan, and add 1lb of sugar for each pint of liquid. Bring to the boil and simmer gently till set.
5. Test on the cold saucer by dripping on some jelly, allowing it to cool briefly and pushing it with a finger. If the jelly wrinkles, pot up in the jars, and cover with lids or jam-jar covers.
6. The finished jelly is good to eat with hot buttered toast, scones, or as an accompaniment to cold lamb or chicken.

For more detailed information on hedgerow food, see Richard Mabey's classic *Food for Free*, or *Hedgerow: River Cottage Handbook No.7* by John Wright.

you can profit by 200 per cent on your original investment if the value of the house rises by £20,000, but a corresponding fall in the value will leave you £10,000 in negative equity, meaning you owe the lender more than the house is worth.

As anyone who has tried to come up with an infallible gambling system will know, there is no such thing as the perfect 'hedge'. You can design something like a Martingale system for roulette, which involves betting on red, and doubling your bet after every losing bet until you win, at which point you start again. Given an infinite pot of money, this strategy would work – but in practice a long run of blacks will eventually wipe out anyone who attempts to use it.

Gambling systems appear to work (at least for a while) because they concentrate all the risk into one relatively improbable outcome. A Martingale gambler might win £1 on each of 99,999 occasions, but then lose £100,000 or more on the one combination that undoes the strategy. This is essentially what happened in 2007–8. The strategies of investment bankers and hedge funds came unstuck when house prices (in the US and elsewhere) started to fall, leaving them with investments and debt instruments that were worth less than the assets they were secured against. Since they had assumed that this was a one in a million chance, they had loaded a huge amount of risk onto that one outcome.

Politicians could have prevented this, or at least reduced the impact, by regulating financial firms and consumer lending more effectively. However many of them were owners of multiple homes – parliamentary expenses in the UK could be used to pay the mortgage on a second home, and MPs could keep the profit from the sales of those properties. Unsurprisingly, with a few honourable exceptions, they failed to notice the fact that allowing house prices and debt to get out of control was not in the general interest. The problem might not have been solved in any case – debt bubbles are seductive as they make a lot of people feel magically richer and it is common for participants to come up with justifications for why it is 'different this time'. However, if our media and politicians had not had so many vested interests in property, there might at least have been a few more voices raising concerns about booming asset prices and financial deregulation.

When the inevitable financial crisis arrived, the banks were bailed out with huge amounts of new money pumped into the system to shore up asset prices. As a result most ordinary people were impoverished as their earnings and savings were devalued, and tax rises and spending cuts in the future became inevitable. Many also had to face up to the possible loss of their homes – the hedges and fences around our homes give us a feeling of security, even when they are owned by banks or landlords, but this security can evaporate all too easily.

Let's agree that the aspiration to make money is in general a positive thing for society, as it provokes entrepreneurial endeavour and creative ideas. But when that aspiration relies on impoverishing others, it becomes a negative. That was essentially the problem of the enclosures – the landowners who profited did so to the detriment of most of the original commoners. It is also the reason why it is morally dubious for hedge funds to push up global food and oil prices by gambling on futures. And it is the root problem with the financial innovations, casino banking and easy credit that led to the credit crunch.

So, who are the true descendants of those low types in the countryside who plied their trade beneath hedgerows? The financiers who gamble trillions of pounds, risking the property and wealth of society in general, the politicians who fail to control them, or the 'common people' who suffer as a result?

I don't believe these financial and political elites have any special entitlement to their wealth and status. Personally I wouldn't want to profit from gambling schemes that impoverish others around me, and I don't think that the few deserve to live in luxury funded by the many.

In the end, I think I would rather be one of the hedge people, speaking hedge and ditch language, and recognising that other people are only the same as me, no better and no worse.

Hatfield's Yew Tunnels

It is in society as in nature – not the useful, but the ornamental that strikes the imagination.

SIR HUMPHREY DAVY

Donato Cinicolo, the hedgelayer (see pages 74–7), has brought me to meet Larry Laird, who spent his working life looking after the hedges, mazes and topiary of Hatfield House. Larry's is the first name on the hedgelaying trophy in Donato's front room, having been the winner of the inaugural competition back in 1986. He has recently retired and lives in the gatehouse to the old vineyard.

In the 1980s, Larry personally planted Hatfield's knot garden, with its fine maze and topiaries. He laid the bricks, which were recycled from a demolished bothy in the grounds, by hand. The site of the garden was originally covered by a wing of the house which was devastated by a fire in the early nineteenth century. The final result has the feel of a Renaissance formal garden. He also tended the much larger yew maze in the east garden, which is a Victorian creation.

We approach Larry's cottage through the woods. Visiting him feels like taking a step back into a lost age. The peacocks and chickens that he breeds fuss around us as we arrive. We sit by an open fire talking about the foxes and badgers that manage to invade Larry's garden from time to time – he has recently lost several peahens to the foxes.

The vineyard, which is now a private garden, used to have arched avenues of yew trees, cut to resemble a series of hedged walls, with towers and battlements. Samuel Pepys often came to Hatfield, writing in his diary in 1661 of a visit to the vineyard:

> [It] is now a very beautiful place again, and then through all the gardens such as I never saw in all my life, nor so grand flowers, nor so great gooseberries, as large as nutmegs.

Yew tunnels and other arbours were popular in this period, both as shaded places where ladies could promenade without risking their pale complexions in the sun and as locations for political intrigue.

For the last three decades, Larry has been attempting to recreate the lost yew tunnels. At the end of our visit he shows me the results of his efforts, dense parallel rows of yew trees that are gradually fusing into hedges. Yew grows slowly, and only about a third of the trees have reached the point where they can be trained to meet overhead – the others still form a vertical corridor. The avenues will eventually become arched, covered walks. However, it will take many more years for it to be complete.

'I won't live to see this finished,' says Larry. 'It will be for someone else to see that through.'

When I ask if he finds that frustrating, his reply is phlegmatic. 'Trees live longer than people. You always have to remember that when you're working with them.'

I tend to think of gardening and hedgemaking as a battle against nature, in which you can only win temporary, individual victories, but Larry has a more harmonious way of

Topiary hedges in the Hatfield garden.

thinking. He is patiently working with nature, accepting its patterns, and trying to mould them. If he can play his part in persuading the trees to grow to his design, then that will be enough for him, even if he doesn't see the results himself.

The same attitude can be seen in a farmer clearing a field or planting saplings for a hedge around it, or a gardener who lays out a formal garden to be enjoyed by their descendants. These acts involve a similar acceptance of being part of a longer term process, something bigger than yourself.

Creating a proper hedge, topiary or formal garden takes time and commitment. In a lazier, less patient world where gardening is represented on television by instant makeover shows, and where municipal gardening often lapses into hedgelike objects, we are in danger of losing our appreciation of slower approaches.

And, of course, the ability to take the longer view lies at the heart of 'heritage' and 'conservation'. Those who work to protect rural hedgerows from extinction, or who preserve the achievements of gardeners who came before them, aren't doing it for personal gratification or immediate results.

What the conservationists, hedgelayers, formal gardeners and topiary enthusiasts I have met share with Larry is that they are happy to play their patient, unegotistical part in a long, slow tradition. It is thanks to the hard work of such people that we have such a rich heritage of hedgerows and gardens to preserve in the first place.

15. State of the Nation
The Future of Hedge Britannia

Hast not thou made an hedge about him, and about his house, and about all that he hath on every side? Thou hast blessed the work of his hands, and his substance is increased in the land.

JOB 1:10

Bourton-on-the-Hill is a charming Cotswold village with a church and pub on the peak of the hill, and the sandy stone buildings that are so typical of the area. I'm visiting Robin Dale, chairman of the National Hedgelaying Society, to discuss the state of the nation's hedges.

The post-war years were difficult ones for hedgerows, and the art of hedgelaying was in decline. From the late 1940s, *Farmers Weekly* responded to this by running annual 'Spring Demonstrations', where agricultural arts including hedge-laying were celebrated. Some of these continued as local events, and were eventually absorbed into the National Hedgelaying Society when it was founded in the 1970s.

Robin regularly acts as a judge at the National Hedge-laying Championships, the culmination of a series of local heats. The contestants have five hours to lay a ten-metre section of hedge – the results are assessed for the precision and quality of the work, and then a year later they are revisited to see how well they have regrown, since this is the ultimate test of a successfully laid hedge.

He has worked on the same farm since 1962, and took over the tenancy from his parents in 1984. Today he mostly grows corn – a few years ago he made the decision to give up on cattle because the price of milk had fallen too low to be profitable.

He has an infectious enthusiasm for the history of his farm, and gives regular farm walks on which he shows visitors the fields, hedges and other features. He has copies of the Luftwaffe aerial photographs of the area, which give a clear view of the ridges and furrows, remnants of the pre-enclosure layout of the fields. When we put this alongside a colour-coded map of the old field names and the allocation of the Manor Farm strips from 1821 you can clearly see which fields were held in common from their ridged pattern.

He is intrigued by the question of how the original strips were allocated. Since the origins of ridge and furrow farming are not fully understood by historians, it is impossible to know how the decisions were made, but each commoner seems to have ended up with a well-chosen mix of good and bad ground – the complex allocation accounts for details such as soil quality, the dampness of the field and the slope of the land. (The farm is on the edge of the lowland Warwickshire clay and the stone belt of the Cotswolds, so the higher ground is harder to farm.)

The enclosures, which came here in two acts in 1733 (for Bank Farm) and 1821 (for Manor Farm), relied on draughtsman's maps that simply drew straight lines across the land

– from the aerial photographs you can see where the old curved ridges continue from one side of the enclosure hedges to the other.

In general the farm is a historical treasure trove. It contains two ancient tithe barns, another farm building that dates to 1453, and the track by the house is a burial road by which the dead were taken to the next village during a period when Bourton's church was unconsecrated. From the highest point of the farm, you can see the old ridges in the lower fields with the naked eye, and also a series of oak trees planted by Lord Redesdale (whose descendants would include the Mitford sisters) – these were part of a patriotic tree-growing drive. Nelson and others were publicly fretting that there were not enough mature oaks to sustain British naval power in the Napoleonic wars. Such trees are now known as 'Napoleonic oaks'.

Robin also tells me of the drovers' road that passes nearby on the rocky hills. For centuries this was the route by which cattle were brought from Tregaron in West Wales into England – the road went over the Cambrian Mountains to Abergwesyn, through the Irfon Valley to Llanwrtyd Wells and Llanafanfawr and onto Painscastle in Powys. From there it went close to Hereford and Cheltenham and on towards London, with the final destination being Barnet Fair, on the northern fringe of London.

Given special metal shoes by the drovers, the cattle would travel between seven and fifteen miles a day. The drovers had a mixed reputation as they often took animals on credit, promising to pay on their return, and the promises weren't always honoured. But they were a hugely important part of the Welsh economy as they brought money in from over the border.

Drovers' roads follow ancient routes. For instance Sewstern Lane, also known as the Drift, runs on the boundary of Lincolnshire and Leicestershire, and was in continuous use from the Bronze Age until the last century. You can partially trace it on aerial imaging – some sections have been turned into roads, in others it is still a hedged green lane (as in a section near to Dry Doddington), and elsewhere you can see the route crossing more recent fields that have interrupted it.

The road near Robin's house dates at least to the fourteenth century and probably earlier. Drovers' roads are characteristically wide (to accommodate a herd or flock) – where modern roads have been built on their route, you tend to see unusually wide verges. They are also often hedged. The hedges were created by those who owned land adjacent to the road to keep the animals out (and the drovers themselves). So drovers' hedges are often of medieval origin.

Robin tells me that pine trees are found along many drovers' roads – he thinks they were probably used as waymarkers. (It has also been suggested that they were planted as a sign to homeless Scots after the Highland Clearances and indicated a sympathetic household, though this seems a less likely story given how long it takes for a pine to grow.)

Drovers called a place where they spent the night a 'castle' and many local placenames such as Jackdaw's Castle, Pomfret Castle and Castle Farm in Deddington probably refer to these, rather than to real castles. On Robin's map of the old field names there is one thin slice of a field called The Slingets, which simply means a long narrow field. It would have served as an overnight holding pen for the drovers' animals.

The State of our Hedgerows

After touring the farm, we settle down to discuss the current condition of Britain's hedgerows. We now have legislation (currently the Hedgerows Regulations, 1997) that prevents their unauthorised removal, and this has stemmed the post-war tide of destruction. But on its own this legislation won't save our rural hedgerows if they are not properly maintained. I am particularly worried by how many are simply being allowed to grow out across the countryside.

This is in spite of increased awareness of their importance. Agricultural hedges today are valued for a variety of practical reasons – they act as a barrier that mitigates soil loss, both in flat areas such as the Fens, where the wind blows surface soil away, and in other areas where water run-off is the problem. By slowing the flow of heavy rain water, they also work as a flood defence, a matter of great importance in areas that have seen flooding in recent years.

Hedges also help to absorb pollution, and collectively play a role in taking greenhouse gases out of the atmosphere. While they are not quite the equivalent of a British rain-forest, they have an important part to play with regard to climate change (and this is equally true of garden hedges in both town and country).

In addition, their contribution to biodiversity is invaluable, because of the flora and fauna they sustain. There are plant species which are rare outside of hedges, for instance the Plymouth pear which can only be found in two hedges in the south-west. Rare and threatened animals that are largely dependent on hedges and hedge borders for their habitats include the brown hairstreak butterfly, the greater horseshoe bat and the cirl bunting. Dormice, which have declined by over 60 per cent since the 1970s, usually live in a dense shrub layer with plenty of undergrowth, and find this environment most easily today in hedges. The Suffolk Wildlife Trust recently announced plans to plant a network of hedges specifically designed to provide a home for dormice.

More common species such as sparrows and bees (and other birds and pollinating insects) can also be encouraged by the maintenance of good hedgerows and hedge margins which provide them with shelter or sustenance.

In spite of all these known virtues, it is clear that there is an ongoing problem with the management of existing hedges. In 2007, less than half of surveyed British hedges were classified as being in good condition. The length of managed hedges fell between 1998 and 2007 by over 5 per cent, while lines of trees increased.

The clear conclusion is that hedgerows are being left to grow out, in spite of government and local grants for hedgelaying. Hedge maintenance is an expensive process – many farmers these days choose to use either the flail or saws mounted on a cutting bar to trim the hedge. Others simply give up on maintaining their hedges. This is a particular issue in areas where the hedges don't need to be laid for the purposes of stock-proofing, and the problem has thus been exacerbated by the recent decline in livestock farming. In parts of the country there have also been experiments with an instant hedging process involving half-cutting through the stems of trees and using a JCB to shove the trees over. Robin is sceptical that this rather brutal shortcut is of much value for hedge preservation.

A hedgerow in East Lothian, trimmed but gappy.

Meanwhile, the proportion of healthy hedgerow trees is also falling – Jon Stokes of the Tree Council reports that the age profile of existing hedgerow trees means that older examples are gradually dying or being felled, while there are too few replacements. The use of the flail is a particular problem here – while most operators are careful to avoid damaging full-grown trees, fewer younger trees are being allowed to grow to maturity than in the past. (To remedy this problem, the English Hedgerow Trust recommends marking some younger saplings with fluorescent tape in order to identify them for protection, so that they are allowed to grow to maturity.) There are about two million hedgerow trees in Britain, but a third of these are already over a century old – many of these have only survived because they used to be pollarded regularly, which prolongs a tree's life.

Common species of hedgerow tree include oak, ash, willow and poplar. The elm population has of course been decimated by Dutch Elm Disease – elm still suckers in the hedgerows, but the trees usually become diseased once they reach a certain height. Robin remembers laying whole hedges of elm in his early days as a hedgelayer, something that few modern British hedgelayers will have been able to experience. (Elm was an especially common hedgerow tree in the Midlands and thus acquired the nickname 'Warwickshire Weed'.)

There are other potential problems to be faced. Industrialised agricultural processes, including the use of herbicides

Robin Dale has been using this favourite billhook since 1964 – it is a bit worn down, but still ferociously sharp.

and fertilisers that can drift into hedgerows, are still inflicting damage. And future enemies of the flora and fauna of hedges may include GM crops, whose effects on other species remain largely unknown.

Journey's End

There are many reasons to be concerned for the future of our hedgerows. But there are also some causes for cautious optimism.

As someone in regular contact with many hedgelayers, Robin assures me that hundreds of miles of hedges are laid each year. Many farmers spend thousands of pounds a year simply on trimming their hedges to keep them in shape. He believes that over 90 per cent of farmers keep their land and hedges in good condition, saying that farmers grow up seeing themselves as guardians of the land – for him this means that 'we try to leave the land in the same condition we find it in – or in better condition'. He describes farmers as gardeners on a larger scale, and points to the many small acts of tidying up and 'weeding' they undertake on a regular basis to help look after the land, for instance grubbing out patches of elder.

One of Robin's responsibilities is representing the National Hedgelaying Society on Hedgelink. This partnership brings together various bodies with an interest in hedges, including the National Farmers' Union, Natural England, the Tree Council, the RSPB and even the Bat Conservation Trust. While it sounds a slightly eccentric quango, it is reassuring to see how much ongoing care and attention is being voluntarily given to looking after our hedgerows.

The art of hedgelaying still survives, although as we've seen, it is dependent on the enthusiasm of a relatively small group of hedgelayers and the patronage of landowners and farmers. But the ongoing enthusiasm and commitment of our professional and amateur hedgelayers suggests that this ancient art will be passed down to future generations.

Robin does suggest one simple political action that would help to preserve our hedgerows. Currently there are two different government schemes encouraging good environmental practice to which farmers can belong. The schemes, which are administered by Natural England, are called Entry Level Stewardship (ELS) and Higher Level Stewardship (HLS). Subsidies for hedgelaying are only available to HLS members, a scheme that is restricted to certain landscapes and areas, such as heathland, moorland, coastal land, wetland and small woodlands, especially where these exist on or adjacent to Sites of Special Scientific Interest.

It would cost money to extend hedgelaying subsidies to members of the more common scheme, the ELS, but this would be a simple and effective way to direct help to hedgerows in all areas, and to foster the art of hedgelaying.

These are difficult economic times, but if as a nation we are going to place obligations on farmers as stewards of the land, it is only reasonable that we sometimes share the costs involved. Hedgelaying is not a cheap or easy process, but it makes a big difference to our environment.

The rural landscape faces many challenges, and it is crucial that farmers, landowners, government agencies and ecologists continue to focus on the importance of hedgerows if we are to avoid further decline. But I leave Robin's farm knowing that there are plenty of people in Britain who do understand the importance of hedges and are working hard to preserve them. In spite of the difficulties they face, this gives me some hope for the future.

As my train trundles back homewards, I look out of the window as we pass through the old kingdom of Wessex. It's a Sunday in August, towards the end of a rainy, humid summer and the entire countryside seems to consist of lush hedgerows and unkempt rows of trees. The landscape has responded to the recent rainfall and warmth with unchecked, exuberant growth.

The future is uncertain. But today at least I can be sure that I still live in a land of hedges.

Bibliography

Adam, David, 'Leylandii may be to blame for house sparrow
decline, say scientists', *Guardian*, 20 November 2008

Allen, Vanessa, 'Mother's joy after winning 24-year battle to get
neighbour to cut 50ft leylandii', *Daily Mail*, 16 May 2008

Blaikie, Francis, *A Treatise on Hedges and the Management
of Hedgerow Timber*, 1821

Bryson, Bill (intro.), *The English Landscape*, Profile, 2000

Cahill, Kevin, 'Who Really Owns Britain?', *Country Life*,
16 November 2010

Chesterton, G. K., *What's Wrong with the World*, Dodd,
Mead & Co., 1910

Cobbett, William, *The American Gardener*, Co Clement, 1821

Cobbett, William, *The English Gardener*, [the author], 1829

Cohu, Will, 'Leylandii: Most planted and most hated garden
tree', *Daily Telegraph*, 1 September 2007

Deakin, Roger, *Wildwood: A Journey Through Trees*,
Penguin, 2008

DEFRA Hedgerow Survey Handbook, DEFRA, 2007

Elliott, Charles (ed.), *The Quotable Gardener*, Lyons
Press, 1991

Fitzherbert, John, *The Book of Husbandry*, 1534

Foulkes, N., *County Monaghan Hedgerow Survey Report*,
Monaghan County Council, 2010

Graham, Kathryn V., 'The Devil's Own Art: Topiary in
    Children's Fiction', *Children's Literature* (vol. 33), Johns
    Hopkins University Press, 2005

Granta 90: Country Life, Granta, 2005

Hanley, Lynsey, *Estates: An Intimate History*, Granta, 2008

Higgins, Rose Standish, *English Pleasure Gardens*, David R.
    Godine, 2003

Hoskins, W. G., *The Making of the English Landscape*, Hodder
    & Stoughton, 1955

Huxley, Anthony, *An Illustrated History of Gardening*,
    Paddington Press, 1978

Jacobs, Joseph, *English Folk Tales*, Forgotten Books, 2010

Jacobs, Joseph, *More English Folk Tales*, Abela, 2009

Jefferies, Richard, *Field and Hedgerow*, Longmans & Co.,
    1889

Jekyll, Gertrude, *The Gardeners Essential*, Robinson, 1991

King, Angela and Sue Clifford, *A Manifesto for Fields*,
    Common Ground, 1997

Leamy, Edmund, *Irish Fairy Tales*, Forgotten Books, 2010

Le Blond, A., *The Theory and Practice of Gardening*, 1712

Mabey, Richard, *Flora Britannica*, Chatto & Windus, 1998

Mabey, Richard, *Food for Free*, Collins, 1972

Matless, David, *Landscape and Englishness*, Reaktion
    Books, 1998

Menneer, Robin, *Prehistoric Hedges in Cornwall*,
    http://www.cornishhedges.co.uk/PDF/prehistoric.pdf, 2007

Morton, A. L., *A People's History of England*, Lawrence
    & Wishart, 1985

Moxham, Roy, *The Great Hedge of India*, Robinson, 2002

Perényi, Eleanor, *Green Thoughts*, Modern Library, 2002

Pollard, E., M. D. Hooper and N. W. Moore, *Hedges*, William Collins, 1974

Poulsen, Charles, *The English Rebels*, Journeyman, 1984

Rackham, Oliver, *The History of the Countryside*, Phoenix, 2000

RHS, *Hedges (RHS Practicals)*, Dorling Kindersley, 2002

Robinson, William, *The Wild Garden*, 1870

Rowe, W. H., *Trees and Shrubs*, Penguin, 1951

Sackville-West, Vita, *Vita Sackville-West's Garden Book*, Atheneum, 1983

Solnit, Rebecca, *Wanderlust*, Verso, 2006

Stein, Sara, *My Weeds*, University of Florida Press, 2000

Stuart, Rory, *Gardens of the World*, Frances Lincoln, 2010

Thomas, Eric and John T. White, *Hedgerow*, Dorling Kindersley, 1983

Thoreau, Henry David, *Journal of Henry David Thoreau*, 1906 (the quote on page 30 is from the entry for 12 February 1851)

Trevelyan, G. M., *English Social History*, Longmans, Green & Co., 1948

Triggs, H. Inigo, *Garden Craft in Europe*, Jeremy Mills, 2008

Uglow, Jenny, *A Little History of British Gardening*, Chatto & Windus, 2004

Walpole, Horace, *On Modern Gardening*, Pallas Athene Arts, 2004

Wheeler, David (ed.), *Penguin Book of Garden Writing*, Penguin, 1998

Wright, John, *Hedgerow (River Cottage Handbook)*, Bloomsbury, 2010

www.cornishhedges.co.uk, for a wealth of detail on
    Cornish hedges
www.hedgelaying.org.uk, the National Hedgelaying Society
    website
www.frostatmidnight.co.uk, the Frost at Midnight
    topiary website

... and the Hedge Britannia blog
hedgebritannia.wordpress.com

Picture Credits

p. 6 © Betsy Barker.

pp. 15, 179 © Greg Heinimann.

pp. 28, 29, 45, 75, 78 (both), 92, 124, 128 © Donato Cinicolo.

p. 143 © Matthew Bullen. Reproduced by permission of
Chatsworth Settlement Trustees.

p. 183 © Duncan Proudfoot.

p. 233 © Jekka McVicar.

p. 241 (top) © Diana Boston.

Plate section credits

Plate 1 © Matthew Bullen. Reproduced by permission of
Chatsworth Settlement Trustees.

Plates 4, 5, 7, 15 © Donato Cinicolo.

Plate 8 (bottom) © Gavin Hogg.

Plate 9 reproduced by permission of Hidcote Manor Garden.

Plate 12 © Charles Hawes.

All other photographs © Hugh Barker.

Acknowledgments

I couldn't have written this book without drawing on the expertise and knowledge of others. In no particular order, I am grateful to: Robin Dale, Jon Stokes, Donato Cinicolo, John Treanor, John Smith and HAWCS, Carl from the Bracknell Forest Rangers, Anthony Blagg, Zac Monroe, Mary Perry, Roger Parris, Robin Menneer, Larry Laird, Michael and Barbara Williams, Pat and Richard Oldale, Eryl Humphrey Jones, Jack and Tom in Burgess Hill, Jekka McVicar, Kathryn V. Graham, Diana Boston, Geof Littlewood at the Bliss Lane Nursery, Tim Sparks, Leo Hollis, Duncan Proudfoot, Patrick Walsh, Richard Atkinson (for explaining the difference between the wood and the trees), Natalie Hunt, Xa Shaw Stewart, everyone at Bloomsbury, Caroline Knight, Stuart Miller (for pointing me towards Robert Frost), Richard Stribley, Chris Crowder, the National Hedgelaying Society, the Credit Crunch posters, Neil Foulkes and the Hedge Laying Association of Ireland, Roy Moxham, Susannah Walker, Chris Maynard (for telling me about Clipsham), Al Barker, Vanessa Smith, Duncan Proudfoot, the owners of the hedges I've photographed, Sally Antony, Hedgeline, Naomi King Li, Ian McNeil Cooke, Gavin Hogg, the Cotley Hunt hedgelayers and Betsy Barker for the many additional pictures and help. And apologies to anyone I've forgotten to mention or who got left out of the final draft.

Index

Page numbers in *italic* refer to the illustrations

A Note on the Author

Hugh Barker has been a bookseller, musician, fruit picker, barman, publisher and writer, amongst other things. He currently lives in North London with his wife, daughter and several cats, surrounded by a small hedge that he can call his own.

A Note on the Type

The text of this book is set in Minion. This typeface was created in 1990 by Robert Slimbach, who based it on the serifed styles of the late Renaissance period. Its name comes from the traditional classification for font size; according to this system, it lies between the sizes nonpareil and brevier. The elegance and versatility of Minion mean that it has now become a design classic.